FlyHigh 4 Fun Grammar Contents

1 Present simple and present continuous
Present simple

We use the present simple to talk about facts and to talk about things we do regularly.
> I like animals.
> We go to school every day.

- We often use these time expressions with the present simple:
to say when something happens:
> at seven o'clock, at night, at the weekends
> in summer, in August, in the morning/afternoon/evening
> on Saturday/Sunday
- to say how often something happens:
> every day/week/year

Look! Spelling rules
We add -s to most verbs for he/she/it in affirmative sentences.
> I read → he reads

For verbs ending in consonant + -y: we change -y to -i and add -es.
> I carry → he carries

For verbs ending in -o we add -es.
> I go → he goes

For verbs ending in -ch, -sh, -ss, -s or -x we add -es.
> I watch → he watches

Affirmative
I/You/We/They read.
He/She/It reads.

Negative
I/You/We/They don't read.
He/She/It doesn't read.

Questions
Do I/you/we/they read?
Does he/she/it read?

Short answers
Yes, I/you/we/they do.   No, I/you/we/they don't.
Yes, he/she/it does.   No, he/she/it doesn't.

Wh- questions
What do I/you/we/they read?
What does he/she/it read?

---

1 **Write the correct form.**

1 Dad ......_washes_...... (wash) his car on Sunday.

2 I .... (not have) lunch at two o'clock.

3 .... (he/go) to school in summer?

4 I .... (do) my homework every day.

5 She .... (not teach) English.

6 .... (you/work) in a shop?

7 Mum .... (watch) TV at night.

8 We .... (play) tennis every week.

2 **Look and write.**

Saturday	Mark	Lisa	Kelly and Jack
morning	play basketball	watch TV	play computer games
afternoon	visit grandma	meet friends	go shopping

1 ___Does___ Mark ___visit___ his grandma in the morning?

___No, he doesn't.___ He visits his grandma ___in the afternoon.___

2 _____ Lisa _____ TV in the afternoon?

_____ . She _____ TV _____ .

3 _____ Kelly and Jack _____ shopping in the afternoon?

_____ . They _____ shopping _____ .

4 _____ Mark _____ basketball in the morning?

_____ . He _____ basketball _____ .

5 _____ Lisa _____ her friends in the afternoon?

_____ . She _____ her friends _____ .

6 _____ Kelly and Jack _____ computer games in the afternoon?

_____ . They _____ computer games _____ .

We use adverbs of frequency to say how regularly we do things.
● always ◐ usually ◑ sometimes ○ never
Adverbs of frequency go before the main verb.
They go after the verb be.
They go before the main verb in questions.
The adverbs always and usually go between
don't/doesn't and the verb in negative sentences.

I always go to bed early.
She is always helpful.
Do you always watch TV?

I don't always have breakfast.

---

3 **Write.**

1 I walk to school. (always)   ___I always walk to school.___

2 We go on holiday in winter. (never)   _____

3 She is helpful. (sometimes)   _____

4 We don't get up early on Sunday. (usually) _____

5 Do you play tennis after school? (always)   _____

6 They are angry. (never)   _____

1 Present continuous

We use the present continuous to talk about things that are happening now.

I'm doing my homework

We use these time expressions with the present continuous:

now, at the moment, today

Look! Spelling rules

We add -ing to all verbs.

read → reading

For verbs ending in -e we take away the -e and then add -ing.

make → making

For verbs ending in one vowel + consonant we double the consonant.

swim → swimming

Affirmative

I'm (am) reading.
You/We/They're (are) reading.
He/She/It's (is) reading.

Negative

I'm not (am not) reading.
You/We/They aren't (are not) reading.
He/She/It isn't (is not) reading.

Questions

Am I reading?
Are you/we/they reading?
Is he/she/it reading?

Short answers

Yes, I am.   No, I'm not.
Yes, we/you/they are   No, we/you/they aren't.
Yes, he/she/it is.   No, he/she/it isn't.

Wh- questions

What am I doing?
Where are you/we/they going?

---

④ **Write the correct form.**

Emma: Hi, Jake. What (**1**) ___are you doing___ (you/do) today?
Jake: Oh, hi, Emma. I (**2**) _____ (work) on my laptop.
Emma: (**3**) _____ (you/do) that project for school?
Jake: Yes, (**4**) _____ . Paul is here.
He (**5**) _____ (help) me.
Emma: Oh, no. Paul is lazy! (**6**) _____ (he/take) a long time?
Jake: No, (**7**) _____ . He's helpful today!
Emma: Well, Kate and I (**8**) _____ (get ready) for the party.
Jack: Party? Whose party?
Emma: Paul's! It's his birthday today!

Present simple or present continuous

⑤ Look, choose and write.

wash   read   ~~have~~   play

Usually	**Today**	
1	 	Peter usually _____has_____ a guitar lesson. Today he ___'s having___ a piano lesson.
2	 	The girls usually _____ tennis. Today they _____ basketball.
3	 	Betty usually _____ the dishes. Today she _____ the car.
4	 	George and Arthur usually _____ newspapers. Today they _____ books.

⑥ Read, choose and write.

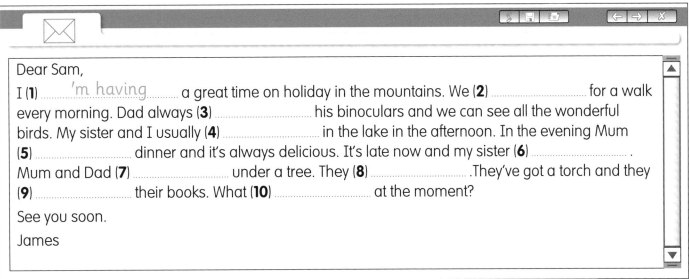

Dear Sam,

I (**1**) ___'m having___ a great time on holiday in the mountains. We (**2**) _____ for a walk every morning. Dad always (**3**) _____ his binoculars and we can see all the wonderful birds. My sister and I usually (**4**) _____ in the lake in the afternoon. In the evening Mum (**5**) _____ dinner and it's always delicious. It's late now and my sister (**6**) _____ . Mum and Dad (**7**) _____ under a tree. They (**8**) _____ .They've got a torch and they (**9**) _____ their books. What (**10**) _____ at the moment?

See you soon.

James

1	have	'm having	are having
2	go	goes	are going
3	take	takes	is taking
4	swim	swims	are swimming
5	cooks	is cooking	doesn't cook

6	sleeps	is sleeping	are sleeping
7	are sitting	sit	am sitting
8	don't talk	aren't talking	isn't talking
9	're reading	read	reads
10	do you do	you are doing	are you doing

2 Adverbs of manner

We use adjectives to describe things and people.
> My father is a quick runner.

We use adverbs of manner to describe actions.
> He runs quickly.

Look! Spelling rules

To make adverbs we usually add -ly to an adjective.
> slow → slowly

For adjectives ending in -y we change the -y to -i and then add -ly.
> happy → happily

Some adverbs are irregular.
> good → well

Adverbs of manner go after the verb or after the verb + object.
> She drives slowly.
> She drives her car slowly.

① Write.

1 I sing very (bad).   I sing very badly.

2 The children are playing (happy).

3 Please carry this box (careful).

4 My grandma walks very (slow).

5 The sun is shining (bright).

6 Sam plays the guitar very (good).

7 William drives his car (fast).

8 Please talk (quiet).

② Match and write.

1 Mrs Brown is a good teacher.

2 Tom is a slow runner.

3 I'm a quick learner.

4 Kate is a brave climber.

5 This is heavy rain.

6 Sam is a bad dancer.

7 You're a quiet singer.

8 Lisa is a clever writer.

a It's raining _____ .

b He dances _____ .

c You sing _____ .

d She climbs _____ .

e She writes _____ .

f He runs _____ .

g She teaches ___ well ___ .

h I learn _____ .

3 Choose and write.

1 quick / quickly

  a My friend walks ___quickly___ .

  b She's a ___quick___ runner, too.

2 good / well

  a My dad sings _____ .

  b He's a _____ dancer, too.

3 careful / carefully

  a You're a _____ driver.

  b You ride your bike _____ , too.

4 quiet / quietly

  a My teacher talks _____ .

  b She's a _____ reader, too.

5 bad / badly

  a My sister dances _____ .

  b She's a _____ singer, too.

6 busy / busily

  a My dad always works _____ .

  b His friends are always _____ , too.

4 What about you? Choose and write.

slow   kind   careful   quick   happy   bad   good   quiet

1 I do my homework _____ .

2 My friend runs _____ .

3 I work _____ .

4 My teacher talks _____ .

5 I ride a bike _____ .

6 My best friend dances _____ .

I run quickly!

5 Write the correct form.

Tigers are amazing animals. They can run very **(1)** ___quickly___ (quick). They can swim **(2)** _____ (good) and they're **(3)** _____ (good) climbers, too. Tigers are very **(4)** _____ (clever) animals. They catch other animals for food. They watch the other animals very **(5)** _____ (careful). They often hide in the grass and they walk very **(6)** _____ (slow). Tigers can move very **(7)** _____ (quiet) so other animals don't hear them. Then they run **(8)** _____ (fast) and catch the other animal before it can run away.

Fun Grammar Review ①

① Choose and write.

Yes, I am.   ~~I'm going to the cinema.~~   I love funny films.   Yes, I do.
Do you want to come with me?   They always start at half past two.

Jake: Hi, Lucy. Are you going to the shops?
Emma: No, I'm not. (**1**) _I'm going to the cinema._
Jake: Do you go to the cinema every Saturday?
Emma: (**2**) .... I love the cinema.
Jake: Are you walking there?
Emma: (**3**) .... I never get the bus.
Jake: What time do the films start?
Emma: (**4**) ....

Jake: I never go to the cinema but I love films. What films do you like?
Emma: (**5**) .... They're great.
Jake: OK. I'm going home now. Have fun at the cinema.
Emma: Wait! (**6**) ....
Jake: Yes, please!

② Write the correct form.

Hi Mark,

How are you? I'm very (**1**) ....excited.... (excited) because I'm in London now! I'm visiting my cousins for a week. I don't know them very (**2**) .... (good) but they sometimes email me. I've got my camera with me. I'm a (**3**) .... (good) photographer and I want to take lots of pictures. I've got my diary, too. Holidays always go very (**4**) .... (quick) and I want to remember every day! London is very (**5**) .... (busy) and there are lots of things to do here. My cousins are very (**6**) .... (kind) and they're taking me to all the best places. We're on the London Eye at the moment. It's a big wheel. It moves very (**7**) .... (slow) and I can see all of London. I'm smiling very (**8**) .... (happy) right now!

See you soon!

Peter

③ Look at Exercise 2. Write yes or no.

1 Peter is in Paris. ....no....
2 Peter is visiting his cousins for a month. ....
3 Peter knows his cousins very well. ....
4 Peter's cousins sometimes email him. ....

5 Peter is a good photographer. ....
6 Peter has got his diary with him. ....
7 London is very quiet. ....
8 Peter is sad now. ....

4 **Write the correct form.**

Dear Tom,
I'm in Spain! It's very hot and sunny and
I **(1)** ....'m enjoying....... (enjoy) my holiday. My
mum and dad **(2)** .... (have) fun at
the moment, too. They usually **(3)** ....
(work) on Friday but now they **(4)** ....
(sit) on the beach. My brother sometimes
(5) .... (play) football with Dad on
Friday but today he **(6)** .... (make)
a sandcastle! I always **(7)** .... (do)
my homework on Friday evening but at the
moment
I **(8)** .... (eat) an ice cream. It's great!
Bye for now.
Maria

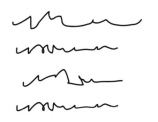

5 **What about you? Answer.**

1 Where do you usually go on holiday? ....

2 Do you like the beach? ....

3 What are you doing at the moment? ....

4 What do you usually do on Fridays? ....

5 Are you eating an ice cream now? ....

6 Are you doing your homework now? ....

My English

You are on holiday. Write a postcard to a friend about what you and your family usually do and what you are doing now.

Dear........................ ,
I'm in .... ! It's .... and I .... my holiday
My .... usually .... on Friday but now
.... My ....
usually .... but today ....
I usually .... but at the moment I ....
Bye for now.
....

3 was, were

The past simple of be is was/were. We often use these time expressions with was/were:

yesterday
last Saturday / week / month / year
in the morning / afternoon / evening
in 1900 / 2008

We were at the beach yesterday. It was very hot.

Affirmative
I/he/she/it was
you/we/they were

Negative
I/he/she/it wasn't (was not)
you/we/they weren't (were not)

Questions
Was I/he/she/it?
Were you/we/they?

Short answers
Yes, I/he/she/it was.
Yes, we/you/they were.

No, I/he/she/it wasn't.
No, we/you/they weren't.

Wh- questions
Where was I/he/she/it yesterday?
Where were you/we/they in the morning?
What was the weather like last week?

① **Look and write** was, wasn't, were **or** weren't.

morning

afternoon

evening

Last Saturday my brother and I (**1**) _____were_____ at the park on our rollerblades. The park is near my uncle's house. In the morning it (**2**) _____ sunny and hot. We (**3**) _____ happy. But in the afternoon it (**4**) _____ sunny. The sky (**5**) _____ cloudy but we (**6**) _____ worried.

In the evening the weather (**7**) _____ stormy and cold. The clouds (**8**) _____ big and black. We (**9**) _____ safe on our rollerblades. 'Let's go to Uncle Dave's house,' I said. Soon, we (**10**) _____ at my uncle's house, with warm clothes and lots of food!

2 **Look at Exercise 1. Write the questions and answers.**

1 it / a sunny morning   Was it a sunny morning?   Yes, it was.

2 the children at home / last Saturday   ....

3 it / sunny in the afternoon   ....

4 the clouds big / in the evening   ....

5 what the weather like / in the evening   ....

6 where / the children all afternoon   ....

> There was/were is the past simple of There is/are.
>
> There was a storm yesterday.
> There weren't lots of people in the park.
> Were there any clouds in the sky?

3 **Look and write** There was, There wasn't, There were **or** There weren't.

A town in 1900.

1 ....There was.......... a big supermarket.

2 .... small shops.

3 .... horses in the street.

4 .... any cars.

5 .... children in the street.

6 .... any mobile phones.

7 .... a theatre.

8 .... a cinema.

4 **Read, choose and write.**

Amy: Hi, Tom. Where (**1**) ..were.. you yesterday?

Tom: I (**2**) .... at the beach with my dogs. They
(**3**) .... happy.

Amy: Oh. (**4**) .... there lots of people at
the beach?

Tom: No, there (**5**) .... It was very quiet.

Amy: What (**6**) .... the weather like?

Tom: It (**7**) .... nice and sunny and there
(**8**) .... any clouds in the sky.

Amy: That's good. (**9**) .... the sea warm?

Tom: No, it (**10**) .... It was very cold!

1 were   was   weren't

2 weren't   were   was

3 were   was   wasn't

4 Was   Were   Weren't

5 weren't   was   wasn't

6 were   wasn't   was

7 was   were   aweren't

8 were   was   weren't

9 Were   Wasn't   Was

10 wasn't   was   weren't

4 Past simple (regular and irregular)
Regular verbs

We use the past simple to talk about actions and events in the past.
   Dad washed the car yesterday.
We often use these time expressions with the past simple:
   yesterday
   yesterday morning/afternoon/evening
   last Saturday/Sunday/week/month/year/summer/winter
   a long time ago

Look! Spelling rules
We usually add -ed to regular verbs.
   walk → walked

For verbs ending in vowel + -y, we add -ed.
   play → played

For verbs ending in -e or -ee we add -d.
   dance → danced

For verbs ending in consonant + -y, we change -y to -i and add -ed.
   cry → cried

For verbs ending in one vowel + consonant, we double the consonant and add -ed.
   stop→stopped

But for verbs ending in two vowels + consonant, we just add -ed.
   wait→waited

Affirmative
I/You/He/She/It/We/They watched TV.

Negative
I/You/He/She/It/We/They didn't watch TV.

Questions
Did I/you/he/she/it/we/they watch TV?

Short answers
Yes, I/you/he/she/it/we/they did.
No, I/you/he/she/it/we/they didn't.

Wh- questions
What did I/you/he/she/it/we/they watch?

① **Say, then write the verbs in the correct boxes.**

   visit   ~~listen~~   wash   skip   follow   want   land   walk   stay

d after b, g, l, m, n, v, w, y, z	**t** after sh/ s / ch / p / k / f	**id** after t and d
listened		

14

② Look, choose and write.

help   live   talk   play   cook   paint   work   not study

A long time ago people (**1**) ...... lived ...... in caves. They (**2**) .... pictures on the walls of their caves. People (**3**) .... food in kitchens. There was a fire in the cave. There weren't any schools then so children (**4**) .... Boys (**5**) .... with their fathers and girls (**6**) .... their mothers. There weren't any toys but young children (**7**) .... lots of games. In the evening people (**8**) .... with their families by the fire.

③ Look at Exercise 2. Write the questions and answers.

1 in houses / live / Did / people .... Did people live in houses? .... No, they didn't. ....

2 paint pictures / people / in caves / Did ....

3 cook / in kitchens / Did / people ....

4 at school / children / Did / study ....

5 help / boys / their mothers / Did ....

6 lots of / Did / have / children / toys ....

7 young children / Did / games / play ....

8 talk / their families / Did / people / with ....

④ Write the correct form.

Emma: (**1**) ...Did you visit... (you/visit) the museum last weekend?

Jake: No, we (**2**) .... We (**3**) .... (decide) to visit the aquarium.

Emma: That's nice. (**4**) .... (you/walk) there?

Jake: Yes, we (**5**) .... It was a long walk but we (**6**) .... (stop) at a café for a cup of tea. The tea was very nice.

Emma: (**7**) .... (you/like) the aquarium?

Jake: Yes, it was great. I (**8**) .... (love) all the wonderful fish. But my sister (**9**) .... (not like) all of it. She was scared of the sharks!

Emma: Oh dear!

Jake: I love sharks! I love dolphins too and in the afternoon I (**10**) .... (watch) the dolphin show. That was really cool.

There are a lot of irregular verbs. Irregular verbs don't form the past simple with -ed. Each irregular verb has a different past simple form.

see → saw	fall → fell
go → went	swim → swam
hear → heard	speak → spoke
have → had	know → knew
drive → drove	take → took

See a full list of irregular verbs on p96.

Affirmative
I/You/He/She/It/We/They went to the park.

Negative
I/You/He/She/It/We/They didn't go to the park.

Questions
Did I/you/he/she/it/we/they go to the park?

Short answers
Yes, I/you/he/she/it/we/they did.
No, I/you/he/she/it/we/they didn't.

Wh- questions
Where did I/you/he/she/it/we/they go?
Who did I/you/he/she/it/we/they go with?

---

5 **Match.**

1 fall
2 go
3 see
4 have
5 read
6 do

a had
b saw
c went
d did
e fell
f read

6 **Write.**

1 sit .... *sat* ....
2 write ....
3 eat ....
4 make ....
5 speak ....
6 sleep ....

7 **Choose and write the correct form.**

go   have   swim   ~~do~~   hear   write   drive   get up

1 I .... *did* .... my homework yesterday evening.

2 We .... to the park last Sunday.

3 Dad .... to work in the car on Monday.

4 You .... an email to your cousin yesterday.

5 They .... a party last weekend.

6 Mum .... at six o'clock yesterday morning.

7 I .... a noise in the garden last night.

8 The children .... in the sea last summer.

I saw a film yesterday.

8 Look and write the correct form.

Our teacher (**1**) ___took___ (take) us to the zoo last Friday. We (**2**) .... (see) lions and gorillas but we (**3**) .... (see) any monkeys. At lunch time we (**4**) .... (go) to a café but we (**5**) .... (have) a picnic on the grass. We (**6**) .... (eat) sandwiches. There were some penguins in the water. We (**7**) .... (throw) bread to the penguins. They (**8**) .... (eat) fish. It was a great day. We had a good time.

9 Look at Exercise 8. Write the questions and answers.

1 the children / go / to a farm / last Friday

Did the children go to a farm last Friday?   No, they didn't. They went to the zoo.

2 the children / see / lions and gorillas

Did the children see lions and gorillas?   Yes, they did.

3 the children / see / monkeys

....

4 the penguins / swim

....

5 the children / have / a picnic

....

6 the children / eat / sandwiches

....

7 the penguins / eat / sandwiches

....

8 the children / have / a good time

....

10 Write the correct form.

Amy: What (**1**) ___did you do___ (you/do) last weekend?

Tom: I (**2**) .... (go) to the beach but I (**3**) .... (not swim) in the sea. I (**4**) .... (make) a sandcastle. Where (**5**) .... (you/go) last Friday?

Amy: We (**6**) .... (not go) out. We (**7**) .... (have) dinner at home. We (**8**) .... (eat) pizza.

4 Regular and irregular verbs

11 **Write the verbs in the correct boxes.**

go   walk   have   play   dance   eat   cry   sit   skip   make
cook   close   do   paint   buy   study   drive   help   sing   fall

Regular verbs
walked

Irregular verbs
went

12 **Write the correct form.**

Dear Lisa,

I had a very bad day yesterday. In the morning I (**1**) ____went____ (go) to the swimming pool with my brother. I (**2**) _____ (take) my towel but I (**3**) _____ (not put) my swimsuit in my bag. My brother (**4**) _____ (swim) but I (**5**) _____ (not go) in the pool. I (**6**) _____ (sit) in the café but I (**7**) _____ (not buy) a drink because I (**8**) _____ (not have) any money with me! In the afternoon I (**9**) _____ (want) to make a cake to surprise my mum. I (**10**) _____ (buy) flour, eggs and milk at the supermarket. Then I (**11**) _____ (walk) home. I saw my friend in the street and I (**12**) _____ (run) to talk to her but I (**13**) _____ (drop) my shopping! It was a mess. I (**14**) _____ (not make) a cake in the end. I (**15**) _____ (not enjoy) my day at all! What about you? (**16**) _____ (you/have) a good day?

Love,

Katie

13 **Look at Exercise 12. Write Did, What, Who or Where and answer.**

1 __Did__ Katie have a good day yesterday?   No, she didn't.
2 __Where__ did she go in the morning?   She went to the swimming pool.
3 _____ she take her towel?
4 _____ did she sit in the morning?
5 _____ did she see in the street?
6 _____ she make a cake?

18

14 **What about you? Write the questions and answers.**

1 what time / you / get up / last Saturday

What time did you get up last Saturday?   I got up at

2 you / go / to the park / in the morning?

Did you go to the park in the morning?   Yes, I did. / No, I didn't.

3 what / you / do / in the afternoon

4 you / watch / TV / in the evening

5 where / you / go / last Sunday

6 what / you / eat / for lunch

7 you / visit / your grandma / in the afternoon

8 who / you / see / in the evening

15 **Choose and write the correct form.**

~~be~~   not know   come   know   start   stop   not have   break

In October 1987 there (**1**) _____was_____ a very big storm in Britain. The storm (**2**) _____ on the 15th of October, late at night. People (**3**) _____ the storm was near but they (**4**) _____ how big it was. First the storm was over the sea. Then it (**5**) _____ to the land. The wind was very fast. This terrible storm (**6**) _____ lots of things. There were trees on the roads and lots of houses (**7**) _____ any electricity. When the storm (**8**) _____ on the 16th October, there was lots of work to do!

16 **Look at Exercise 15. Write yes or no.**

1 The storm was in October 1987.   _yes_

2 The storm started in the morning.   _____

3 People knew how big the storm was.   _____

4 The wind was very slow.

5 The storm broke many things.   _____

6 There were trees on the road.   _____

7 Lots of houses had power after the storm.   _____

8 There was lots of work to do after the storm.   _____

5 Prepositions of place and movement
Prepositions of place

We use prepositions of place to say where people or things are.

on   in   under   behind   next to   in front of

① **Look, choose and write.**

This is my bedroom. There's a ball (**1**) __under__ my bed and there's a CD (**2**) _____ my bed. There's a desk (**3**) _____ my bed. There's a computer (**4**) _____ the desk and there are some flowers (**5**) _____ the computer. There's a bin (**6**) _____ the desk and there's a chair (**7**) _____ the desk. There's a shelf (**8**) _____ the wall. There are some books (**9**) _____ the shelf and there's a radio (**10**) _____ the books. I love my room!

1 under	behind	on
2 on	in	under
3 next to	behind	in
4 in	on	under
5 on	behind	in
6 behind	on	under
7 under	behind	in front of
8 in front of	on	next to
9 in	under	on
10 behind	next to	under

② **Match and circle.**

1 There are lots of fish

2 Children, please sit

3 Your mouth is

4 In the car you sit

5 Who do you sit

6 Our garden is

a under / on your nose.

b in / on the sea.

c in / next to at school?

d on / in front of our house

e in front of / on your chairs!

f behind / under the driver.

Prepositions of movement

We use prepositions of movement to say how people or things are moving.

| across | along | around | past | up | down | into | through |

③ **Read, choose and write.**

1 We go ..<u>past</u>.. the sweet shop every morning but we never go in.　　**a** past　**b** across　**c** along

2 The girls danced in circles .... the tree.　　**a** through　**b** along　**c** around

3 I always look for cars before I walk .... the street.　　**a** across　**b** around　**c** past

4 They stopped talking when the teacher came .... the room.　　**a** up　**b** into　**c** down

5 We walked .... the mountain and had a picnic at the top.　　**a** across　**b** into　**c** up

6 Help! I'm stuck in the tree and I can't climb ....　　**a** through　**b** along　**c** down

④ **Circle.**

Saturday

Dear Diary,
At ten o'clock last night I was in bed. I heard a noise outside and I was very scared. I got up and opened my bedroom door. I walked **(1)** ⟨past⟩ / up my mum and dad's room and then I went slowly **(2)** through / down the stairs to the hall. I quietly walked **(3)** around / along the hall to the kitchen. I opened the kitchen door and I looked **(4)** around / along the room. Just then, my cat jumped **(5)** across / through the kitchen window. I laughed happily and I went **(6)** up / down the stairs to bed again.

⑤ **Look, choose and write.**

around (x2)　along (x2)　through　past　across (x2)

Tom and Maria walk to school every day. Tom leaves his house and he walks **(1)** ....<u>along</u>.... the road.
He goes **(2)** .... the railway station and **(3)** .... the bridge. He goes **(4)** .... the park and then he is at school.

Maria leaves her house and she walks **(5)** .... the road. She goes **(6)** .... the supermarket and **(7)** .... the river. She goes **(8)** .... the castle and then she is at school.

Fun Grammar Review ②

① Choose and write.

I went with my family.   No, there wasn't.   ~~I was in the mountains.~~
No, I didn't.   He swam in the lake.   Yes, we did.

Amy: Hi, Dan. Where were you last weekend?
Tom: (1) _I was in the mountains._
Amy: Did you ski?
Tom: (2) .... I climbed
and I walked.
Amy: Who did you go with?
Tom: (3) ....
Amy: Did your mum and dad climb the mountains?

Tom: My mum climbed with me but my dad didn't
climb. (4) ....
Amy: Where did you stay? Was there a hotel there?
Tom: (5) .... We stayed
at my aunt's house.
Amy: Did you and your family have a good time?
Tom: (6) .... It was
great!

② Write the correct form.

Dear Jenny,
I'm in Paris! It's amazing here. Yesterday morning
I (1) ...... walked ...... (walk) into the city centre with
my mum and dad and we (2) .... (see)
the Eiffel Tower. I (3) .... (take) lots of
photos. We (4) .... (not climb) the tower
because there (5) .... (be) lots of people
there. We (6) .... (have) lunch in a café.
Then we (7) .... (look) in some shops but
I (8) .... (not buy) any souvenirs. In the
evening we (9) .... (listen) to a band
playing in the park. I (10) .... (not go)
to bed early. I went to bed at eleven o'clock!
Bye for now.
Susie

③ Look at Exercise 2. Write yes or no.

1 Jenny walked into the city centre yesterday.   _yes_

2 She saw the Eiffel Tower.   ....

3 Jenny and her parents climbed the Eiffel Tower.   ....

4 There were lots of people at the Eiffel Tower.   ....

5 Jenny had lunch in the park.   ....

6 Jenny bought some souvenirs.   ....

7 They listened to a band in the evening.   ....

8 Jenny went to bed early.   ....

(4) Choose and write.

along   in   on   into   up   see   take   ~~get up~~   have   go

Hi Jake,

How are you? I was on holiday last week. We went to Turkey. We stayed in a hotel. I had a great time. In the morning we **(1)** _got up_ early and **(2)** .... to the beach. We played **(3)** .... the beach and we swam **(4)** .... the sea. It was cold but it was fun! In the afternoon Dad **(5)** .... us out on a boat. We **(6)** .... dolphins in the sea. It was cool! In the evening we went **(7)** .... the town and walked **(8)** .... the river. Then we walked **(9)** .... the hill to a restaurant at the top. There we **(10)** .... pizza every evening.

See you soon!

Peter

(5) What about you? Answer.

1 Where did you go on holiday last year? ....

2 Where did you stay? ....

3 What did you do in the morning? ....

4 What did you do in the afternoon? ....

5 What did you do in the evening? ....

6 What did you eat? ....

My English

You were on holiday last week. Write an email to a friend about what you did.

Dear .... ,

How are you? I was ....
In the morning we ....
In the afternoon we ....
In the evening ....
See you soon!

....

Countable and uncountable nouns
some(body), any(body), no(body)
Countable and uncountable nouns

Countable nouns can be singular or plural. We can count them.

one sandwich two sandwiches three sandwiches

We use singular countable nouns when we are talking about one item.

There's an apple in the bag.

We use plural countable nouns when we are talking about more than one item.

There are three apples in the bag.

Uncountable nouns don't have a plural form. We can't count them.

juice water bread money

We use a/an with singular countable nouns. We use some with uncountable nouns and plural countable nouns.

an apple a peach some orange juice some peaches

① **Write the words in the correct boxes.**

~~milk~~ ~~banana~~ burger orange sugar seat rice chip
carriage pea meat money spaghetti flour luggage cabbage

Countable	Uncountable
banana	milk

② **Write a, an or some.**

1 I had _an_ egg for breakfast this morning.

2 Mum bought _____ bread at the supermarket.

3 I want _____ ticket for the museum please.

4 We saw _____ owl at the farm.

5 Let's put _____ rice in the soup.

6 I'd like _____ strawberries please.

7 He's eating _____ apple.

8 Please buy _____ meat for dinner.

9 I always put _____ sugar in my tea.

10 I only had _____ sandwich for lunch.

some, any, no

We use some, any and no with plural countable nouns and uncountable nouns.

We use some in positive statements.
> There is some milk in the fridge.

We use any in negative statements and questions.
> There aren't any apples in the bowl.
> Is there any flour in the bag?

Look!
We use some in questions with can and in offers.
> Can I have some chocolate, please?
> Would you like some milk?

We use no with the affirmative to give a negative meaning.
> There is no juice in the fridge.
> There are no oranges in the bowl.

③ **Circle.**

1 There isn't (any) / no sugar in the bowl.

2 We've got any / no homework today.

3 Are there any / some strawberries in the fridge?

4 Would you like no / some coffee?

5 Have you got any / some luggage?

6 There are some / any books on the table.

7 There aren't any / no seats on the train.

8 Can I have some / any milk, please?

④ **Write some, any or no.**

Amy: Would you like (**1**) _some_ salad with your burger?

Tom: No, thanks. Can I have (**2**) .... chips, please?

Amy: Did your dad buy (**3**) .... meat yesterday?

Tom: Yes, he did. He wants to make (**4**) .... stew. I hate stew!

Amy: Don't worry! I bought (**5**) .... bread this morning.

Tom: Great! Let's make (**6**) .... sandwiches later.

Amy: OK. But let's cook (**7**) .... spaghetti, too.

Tom: We can't. There is (**8**) .... spaghetti in the cupboard.

6 somebody, anybody, nobody
something, anything, nothing

We use somebody, anybody and nobody to talk about people.
> There's somebody in the garden.

We use something, anything and nothing to talk about things.
> Is there anything in the box?

Look!
We use somebody and something in affirmative statements.
> I've got something in my shoe.
> There is somebody on the phone.

We use anybody and anything in negative statements and questions.
> There wasn't anybody in the park yesterday.
> Have we got anything to eat?

We use nobody and nothing with the affirmative to give a negative meaning.
> There is nobody at the door.
> There is nothing in my bag.

We also use anything to make offers.
> Would you like anything else?

---

⑤ Choose and write.

somebody ~~anything~~ nobody anybody nothing something

1 Did you buy __anything__ nice yesterday?

2 The house's empty. There's _____ here.

3 Listen. There's _____ at the door.

4 I'm thirsty but there's _____ to drink.

5 I've got _____ to show you. A new car!

6 Hello? Is there _____ there?

⑥ Rewrite correctly.

1 I'm ill. I can't do ~~something~~ today.   I'm ill. I can't do anything today.

2 Is there ~~nobody~~ in the classroom now? ....

3 I can't buy ~~something~~. I haven't got any money. ....

4 There's ~~anything~~ in this bag. It's empty. ....

5 Listen. I want to ask you ~~nothing~~. ....

6 I heard a noise. I think there's ~~anybody~~ in the garden. ....

7 There isn't ~~something~~ in the fridge. Let's go shopping. ....

8 Here's your tea. Would you like ~~anybody~~ else? ....

7 Read, choose and write.

Jake: Hi, Emma. Are you doing (**1**) _anything_ nice today?

Emma: Yes, I am. I'm going to Anna's party but I've got (**2**) _____ to wear.

Jake: Oh dear. You need (**3**) _____ new clothes.

Emma: I know. I want to buy (**4**) _____ nice for Anna, too but I haven't got (**5**) _____ money.

Jake: I've got an idea. You can make (**6**) _____ for Anna.

Emma: Don't be silly. I can't make (**7**) _____.

Jake: Yes, you can. You can make some sweets. Have you got (**8**) _____ chocolate?

Emma: Yes, I have. I've got (**9**) _____ sugar, too.

Jake: Great! I've got (**10**) _____ to do this morning. I can help you.

Emma: Thanks, Jake!

1	anything	something	nothing
2	anything	nothing	nobody
3	some	any	no
4	anything	something	nothing
5	some	any	no
6	anything	something	nothing
7	anything	something	nothing
8	some	any	no
9	some	any	no
10	nobody	anything	nothing

8 Circle.

1 I don't understand. I need ~~some~~ / something help.

2 Listen. I think somebody / some is calling you.

3 Is there anybody / any at home?

4 The classroom is empty. There's no / nobody here.

5 We're hungry. We'd like some / something pizza.

6 Is there any / anything money in your wallet?

9 Choose and write.

somebody   no   any   ~~something~~   anybody   anything   some   nothing

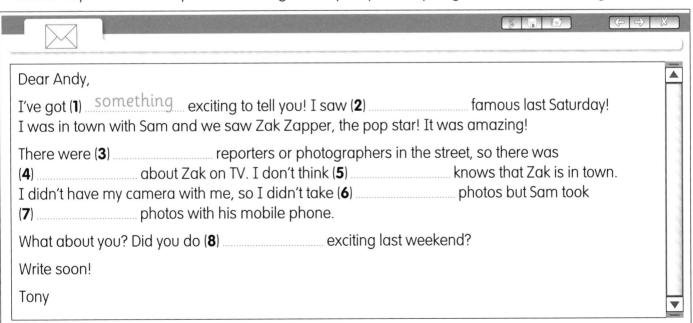

Dear Andy,

I've got (**1**) _something_ exciting to tell you! I saw (**2**) _____ famous last Saturday! I was in town with Sam and we saw Zak Zapper, the pop star! It was amazing!

There were (**3**) _____ reporters or photographers in the street, so there was (**4**) _____ about Zak on TV. I don't think (**5**) _____ knows that Zak is in town. I didn't have my camera with me, so I didn't take (**6**) _____ photos but Sam took (**7**) _____ photos with his mobile phone.

What about you? Did you do (**8**) _____ exciting last weekend?

Write soon!

Tony

7 Quantifiers
many, much, a lot of, a few, a little
How much?, How many?

We use quantifiers to describe amounts.

We use many with plural countable nouns and much with uncountable nouns.
I've got many cousins. There isn't much milk.

We use many and much in questions.
Are there many houses in your street?   Is there much money in your bag?

We use not many and not much in negative sentences to talk about a small amount.
There aren't many cherries in the bowl.   There isn't much butter on my bread.

① **Write much or many.**

1 There isn't _much_ cheese in my sandwich.

2 You haven't got _____ T-shirts.

3 I don't eat _____ chocolate.

4 There aren't _____ children in the park.

5 We don't read _____ books.

6 Are there _____ shops in your street?

7 They haven't got _____ luggage.

8 Is there _____ juice in the fridge?

9 He's got _____ friends.

10 There isn't _____ rice on my plate.

We use a lot of with plural countable nouns and uncountable nouns to talk about a large amount.
I've got a lot of homework.
We use a lot of in affirmative and negative statements and questions.
There are a lot of apples on the table.   There aren't a lot of sweets in the bag.
Is there a lot of milk in the fridge?

We use a few with plural countable nouns talk about a small amount.
There are a few cherries in the fridge.

We use a little with uncountable nouns to talk about a small amount.
There is a little juice in the glass.

② **Write a lot of, a little or a few.**

We haven't got much food in the kitchen. We've only got (**1**) _a few_ peas and only (**2**) _____ meat. There is (**3**) _____ juice in the fridge and there are (**4**) _____ tomatoes. But that isn't enough for two people. We haven't got any bread. But there are (**5**) _____ potatoes. We've got twenty! There is (**6**) _____ milk too – three bottles! So what can we make for dinner?

3 Tick (✔), or cross (✗). Correct the wrong sentences.

1 We haven't got many money. ✗ We haven't got much money.
2 There are a lot of pens in my bag. ✔
3 Is there much milk in the fridge? ☐
4 We've got a few sugar. ☐
5 Are there much flowers in your garden? ☐
6 Can I have a little strawberries, please? ☐
7 Have you got much spaghetti? ☐
8 I've got a little friends. ☐
9 Have you got many luggage? ☐
10 There aren't a lot of seats on the train. ☐

4 Look, choose and write.

many (x3)   much   little   a lot   few   lot of

This is my bedroom. There aren't (1) __many__ posters on the walls in my room but there are a (2) _____ photos of my friends. There's a box on my desk with a (3) _____ money in it. There's a computer on my desk, too. I've got (4) _____ of computer games. I've got a radio but it isn't good so I don't listen to (5) _____ music. I haven't got (6) _____ CDs but I've got a (7) _____ books on my shelf. They're great! Have you got (8) _____ books?

5 What about you? Circle and answer.

1 Are there much / many posters on your wall?   Yes, there are./No, there aren't.
2 Are there a lot of / lot of photos in your room?
3 Is there many / much money in your room?
4 Have you got a lot of / much computer games?
5 Have you got many / much CDs?
6 Have you got a lot / a lot of books?

6 Write the questions and answers.

1 milk

Is there much milk?   No, there isn't.

2 cabbages

Are there many cabbages?   No, there aren't.

3 chocolate

....

4 biscuits

....

5 bread

....

6 tomatoes

....

7 meal

....

8 chips

....

We use How many and How much to ask about numbers and amounts.

We use How many with plural countable nouns.
    How many books have you got?

We use How much with uncountable nouns.
    How much milk is there?

We also use How much to ask about prices.
    How much is this T-shirt? It's €10.

---

7 Look at Exercise 6. Write How much or How many and answer.

1 How many   cabbages are there?   There are two cabbages.
2 How much   chocolate is there?   There is a lot of chocolate.
3 ....   meat is there?   ....
4 ....   biscuits are there?   ....
5 ....   chips are there?   ....
6 ....   milk is there?   ....
7 ....   tomatoes are there?   ....
8 ....   bread is there?   ....

much, many, a lot of, a few, a little, How much? or How many?

⑧ Circle.

Tom: Let's make a cake for my Mum's birthday.
Jake: Good idea. How (**1**) much / many flour have we got?
Tom: We've got a (**2**) lot / lot of flour but we've only got a
(**3**) little / few sugar.
Jake: Oh dear. Have we got a (**4**) few / little eggs?
Tom: We've got two eggs. How (**5**) much / many eggs do we need?
Jake: We need four. Is there a (**6**) lot of / few butter in the fridge?
Tom: There isn't (**7**) much / many butter but there is (**8**) many / a lot of milk.
Jake: OK. Have you got (**9**) a lot of / a few money?
Tom: Yes, I have.
Jake: Good. Let's go to the supermarket. We need (**10**) many / much things!

⑨ Write and match.

1 Have they got much luggage?
2 How .... are the tickets?
3 How .... potatoes do you want?
4 Is there a .... of juice in the fridge?
5 Would you like a .... water?
6 Have you got a .... games?

a No, there isn't.
b No, thank you.
c Two please.
d Yes, they have.
e Five euros each.
f Yes, I have.

⑩ Choose and write.

few   ~~lot~~   many   much   little   of

Dear Paul,

My new house is great. There are a (**1**) ....lot.... of rooms in the house. My favourite room is my bedroom.

My new house is near a beach. There isn't (**2**) .... sand on the beach but it's very pretty. It's very quiet, too. There are never (**3**) .... people there. I go to the beach every day. I take a (**4**) .... food and some water and I have a picnic. I don't know a lot (**5**) .... people here but I'm slowly making a (**6**) .... new friends. I'm very happy.

Write soon!

John

Fun Grammar Review 3

① Circle.

1 How much / (many) glasses do we need?
2 Is there anybody / anything to eat? I'm hungry.
3 I've got a few / little CDs.
4 Harry! There's somebody / nothing on the phone for you.

5 There isn't no / any water in my glass.
6 We haven't got much / many ice cream.
7 There's a few / little money in my bag.
8 Are there some / any chocolate biscuits on the plate?

② Look, choose and write.

somebody   little   few   much   many   lot   ~~something~~   nothing

1 There is _something_ in the bag.
2 There are a .... of sweets in the bowl.
3 There aren't .... flowers in the room.
4 There is .... on the chair.
5 There isn't .... water on the table.
6 There is .... behind the curtain.
7 There are a .... photos on the shelf.
8 There is a .... cheese on the plate.

③ Choose and write.

1 Are there _any_ sweets in the bowl?

   a ~~any~~   **b** some   **c** much

2 There isn't .... in the bag.

   a nothing   **b** anything   **c** some

3 Would you like .... else?

   a any   **b** many   **c** anything

4 I can see .... in our garden.

   a anything   **b** somebody   **c** nobody

5 How .... is that shirt?

   a many   **b** few   **c** much

6 There is a .... juice in the fridge.

   a little   **b** few   **c** lot

(4) Choose and write.

nobody at home   no juice   much fun   lot of milk
little salad   ~~anything yesterday~~

> I didn't cook (**1**) _anything yesterday_ . I ate a (**2**) .... There was
> (**3**) .... so I drank a (**4**) .... In the afternoon
> I phoned my friend but there was (**5**) .... It wasn't an exciting day
> and I didn't have (**6**) ....

(5) Read, choose and write.

Monday

Dear Diary,
I had a great day yesterday. I went to a party. It was a surprise party for my
friend. He didn't know (**1**) _anything_ about it. He was very surprised! There were
(**2**) .... people in his house. I didn't know (**3**) .... people at the
party at first but I quickly made (**4**) .... new friends! The music was
great and I danced. There was a (**5**) .... of great food. I ate sandwiches
and chips. I didn't have (**6**) .... pizza but I had a (**7**) .... birthday
cake. It was delicious. I was tired today, so I didn't do (**8**) .... exciting.
I had a quiet day at home.

1	nothing	something	anything	**5**	lot	little	few
2	many	much	nobody	**6**	some	no	any
3	any	little	few	**7**	little	few	lot
4	some	any	no	**8**	something	anything	nothing

**You went to a party last weekend. Write about it in your diary. Say what you did,
who you met and what you ate at the party.**

Monday

Dear Diary,
I had a great day last Saturday. I went to a party. It was ....
I didn't know .... but I ....
The music was .... and I .... There was ....
I ate .... I didn't have ....
.... , but I had ....
....

8 Possessive adjectives and pronouns
Subject and object pronouns
Possessive adjectives and possessive pronouns

We use subject and object pronouns to talk about people or things without using their names.

We use subject pronouns before the main verb.
    I help my mum every weekend.

We use object pronouns after the main verb and before prepositions.
    I help her.
    Do you want to come with me?

Subject pronouns	Object pronouns
I	me
you	you
he	him
she	her
it	it
we	us
you	you
they	them

① Match.

1 I'm going to the beach this afternoon.
2 You're my best friend.
3 He's singing a lovely song.
4 She's a really great dancer.
5 We've got a new green ball.
6 Look over there! They're thieves!

a Play with us.
b Look at her.
c Stop them!
d I like you.
e Come with me.
f Can you hear him?

We use possessive adjectives and possessive pronouns to say who things belong to.

We use possessive adjectives before a noun. We use possessive pronouns after a noun.

They replace the possessive adjective and the noun.
    This is my bag. It's mine.

Possessive adjectives	Possessive pronouns
my	mine
your	yours
his	his
her	hers
its	–
our	ours
your	yours
their	theirs

② Circle.

1 She's wearing (her) / hers new hat today.
2 That's not your kite. It's our / ours.
3 These CDs are my / mine.
4 This is my brother. His / Her name is John.

5 Is that jacket her / hers?
6 The dogs are sleeping in their / theirs beds.
7 Is this pen my / yours?
8 Dad is in the garden. He's washing his / its car.

3 Choose and write.

1 Mike is riding _his_ new bike.

  a him   **b** ~~his~~   **c** he

2 This fantastic book is ....

  a me   **b** my   **c** mine

3 Good morning. Can I help .... ?

  a you   **b** your   **c** yours

4 Mum's busy. She's washing .... hair.

  a she   **b** her   **c** hers

5 That house over there is ....

  a us   **b** our   **c** ours

6 Is she .... sister or cousin?

  a they   **b** their   **c** theirs

7 You're .... best friend in the class.

  a me   **b** my   **c** mine

8 Who is that? Do .... know him?

  a you   **b** your   **c** yours

4 Choose and write.

her   it   ~~my~~   yours   his   him

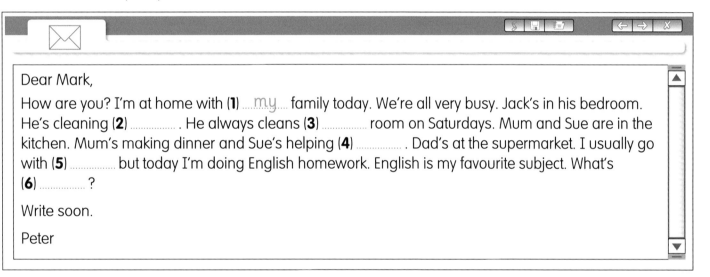

Dear Mark,

How are you? I'm at home with **(1)** _my_ family today. We're all very busy. Jack's in his bedroom. He's cleaning **(2)** .... He always cleans **(3)** .... room on Saturdays. Mum and Sue are in the kitchen. Mum's making dinner and Sue's helping **(4)** .... Dad's at the supermarket. I usually go with **(5)** .... but today I'm doing English homework. English is my favourite subject. What's **(6)** .... ?

Write soon.

Peter

5 Write.

1 I'm not cleaning my bedroom.
  I'm cleaning your bedroom. (you)

2 We aren't playing our computer games.
  .... (they)

3 She isn't talking to you.
  .... (I)

4 This bike isn't his.
  .... (she)

5 They aren't eating their sandwiches.
  .... (we)

6 I'm not writing to her.
  .... (he)

7 Those sweets aren't yours.
  .... (we)

8 I'm not using his pen.
  .... (she)

Whose and possessive *'s*

We use Whose to ask who things belong to.
   Whose jacket is this?

We use the possessive 's to say who things belong to.
   It's Peter's jacket.

We can use the possessive 's without the noun.
   Whose jacket is this? It's Peter's.

(6) **Match and write.**

Amy   Sam   Dan   Lisa   Ben   Ella

1 It's .... *Dan's* .... scarf.   **4** It's .... tie.

2 They're .... gloves.   **5** They're .... trainers.

3 The belt is ....   **6** The jacket is ....

(7) **Look at Exercise 6. Choose and write.**

Whose (x3)   Dan's   Amy's   Sam's

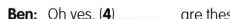

Ben: Look at these clothes. (**1**) *Whose* scarf is this?
Lisa: It's (**2**) .... He bought it last week.
Ben: Oh. Are these (**3**) .... trainers?
Lisa: No, they aren't. Sam isn't wearing any trainers.

Ben: Oh yes. (**4**) .... are these trainers, then?
Lisa: They're (**5**) ....
Ben: There's a jacket here, too. (**6**) .... is it?
Lisa: It's mine silly!

8 **Write the questions and answers.**

 1 my compass — Whose compass is this?

It's mine.

 2 your trainers — Whose trainers are these?

They're

 3 our gloves

 4 her luggage

5 his binoculars

6 their laptop

9 **Read, choose and write.**

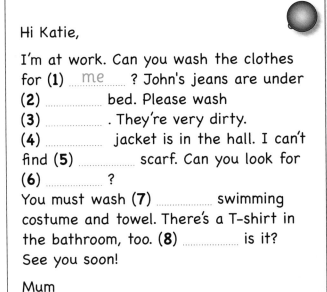

Hi Katie,

I'm at work. Can you wash the clothes
for **(1)** _me_ ? John's jeans are under
(2) _____ bed. Please wash
(3) _____ . They're very dirty.
(4) _____ jacket is in the hall. I can't
find **(5)** _____ scarf. Can you look for
(6) _____ ?
You must wash **(7)** _____ swimming
costume and towel. There's a T-shirt in
the bathroom, too. **(8)** _____ is it?
See you soon!

Mum

1	I	my	me
2	he	his	him
3	them	they	their
4	Emma	Emma is	Emma's
5	me	my	mine
6	it	them	its
7	you	your	yours
8	Who	Who's	Whose

10 **Look at Exercise 9. Complete the questions and match.**

1 _Whose_ jeans are under the bed?   **a** Emma's

2 _____ jacket is in the hall?   **b** Katie's

3 _____ swimming costume is it?   **c** John's

4 _____ scarf is missing?   **d** Mum's

5 _____ jeans are dirty?   **e** Katie's

6 _____ towel is it?   **f** John's

9 Comparatives and superlatives
Comparatives

We use the comparative form of adjectives to compare two people or things.
   Susie is younger than Katie.

Look! Spelling rules

To form the comparative we usually add -er to the end of short adjectives.
   tall → taller

For short adjectives ending in -e we add -r.
   nice → nicer

For short adjectives ending in -y we change the -y to -i and then add -er.
   pretty → prettier

For short adjectives ending in vowel + consonant we double the final consonant.
   big → bigger

We form the comparative of long adjectives with more + adjective.
   My computer was more expensive than yours.

Some adjectives have an irregular comparative form.
   good → better
   bad → worse

① **Write the correct form.**

1 fat   *fatter*

2 dangerous   ....

3 happy   ....

4 good   ....

5 big   ....

6 large   ....

7 small   ....

8 comfortable ....

9 white   ....

10 bad   ....

② **Write.**

1 James / tall / his dad

James is taller than his dad.

2 You / clever / me

3 George / lazy / Stan

4 This film / bad / yesterday's

5 Our dogs / nice / their dogs

6 Your mobile phone / expensive / mine

7 Katie / beautiful / me

8 My mum / thin / my dad

③ Write the correct form.

Pets are great, but sometimes they are hard work. You must always think carefully before you buy a pet. Dogs are usually (**1**) ......*friendlier than*...... (friendly) cats. But dogs are (**2**) .... (noisy) cats, too. Cats are (**3**) .... (quiet) dogs but they are (**4**) .... (noisy) fish. Fish are (**5**) .... (clean) cats and dogs, too. Dogs are usually (**6**) .... (big) cats. They need a garden and they need lots of long walks. Cats are often (**7**) .... (small) dogs but fish are (**8**) .... (easy) cats and dogs. So what's the best pet for you?

④ Match.

1	Bikes are	**a**	than that van.
2	This van is bigger	**b**	cleaner than cars.
3	My scooter is more	**c**	is taller.
4	I'm more excited than	**d**	expensive than yours.
5	This black motorbike	**e**	all the children here.
6	Dave is tall but John	**f**	is newer than that one.

⑤ Look and write the questions and answers.

1 house 1 / pretty / house 2

........*Is house 1 prettier than house 2?*........   ....*No, it isn't. It's uglier than house 2.*........

2 house 2 / ugly / house 1

....

3 house 2 / big / house 1

....

4 house 2 / small / house 1

....

9 Superlatives

We use the superlative form of adjectives to compare three or more people or things.
> John is the youngest boy in the class.

Look! Spelling rules
To form the superlative we use the before the adjective and then usually add -est to the end of short adjectives.
> tall → the tallest

For short adjectives ending in -e we add -st.
> nice → the nicest

For short adjectives ending in -y we change the -y to -i and then add -est.
> pretty → the prettiest

For short adjectives ending in vowel + consonant we double the final consonant.
> big → the biggest

We form the superlative of long adjectives with the most + adjective.
> This is the most expensive computer in the shop.

Some adjectives have an irregular superlative form.
> good → the best
> bad → the worst

6 Write the correct form.

1 wet   the wettest   3 bad ....   5 intelligent ....

2 beautiful ....   4 nice ....   6 silly ....

7 Write the questions. Then choose.

QUIZ TIME!

1 What is ....the highest.... (high) mountain?

   a Mount Everest   **b** Mount Olympus
   c Mount Fuji

2 What is .... (fast) animal?

   a the lion   **b** the tiger
   c the cheetah

3 What is .... (cold) place?

   a Antarctica   **b** Africa
   c Australia

4 What is .... (dangerous) animal?

   a the whale   **b** the mosquito
   c the snake

5 What is .... (long) river?

   a the Amazon   **b** the Danube
   c the Thames

6 What's .... (strong) animal?

   a the monkey   **b** the bear
   c the elephant

1 a   2 c   3 a   4 b   5 a   6 c

8 Write the correct form.

I love sports. I think PE is (1) ....the best........ (good) subject at school. I'm in the school football team and the school basketball team. I'm good at football because I'm (2) .... (fast) person in the team. I'm good at basketball because I'm (3) .... (tall) person in my class. My brother is a great basketball player. He's (4) .... (good) player in our town. He plays for a famous team. He's (5) .... (old) boy in his class but he's (6) .... (young) person in his team. My favourite sport is skiing. Skiing is (7) .... (exciting) sport in the world. I want to ski on (8) .... (high) mountain in the world one day!

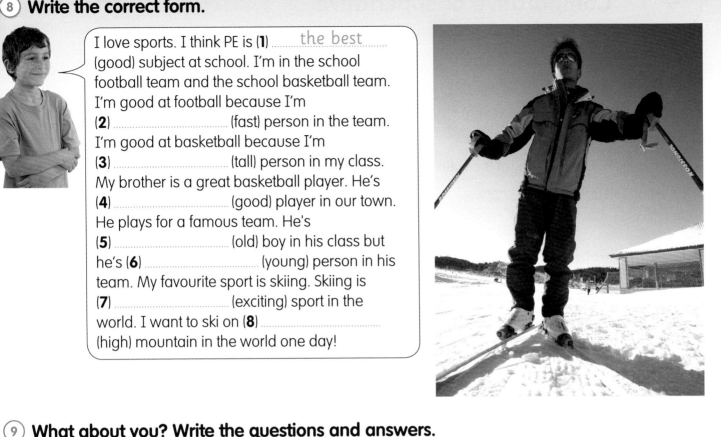

9 What about you? Write the questions and answers.

1 Who is ....the tallest.... person in your school? (tall) .... is the tallest person in my school.

2 Who is .... person in your family? (old) ....

3 What's .... subject at school? (good) ....

4 Who's .... person in your class? (fast) ....

5 Who is .... person in your class? (young) ....

6 What's .... sport in your country? (exciting) ....

10 Tick (✔) or cross (✗). Correct the wrong sentences.

1 Who is the tallest? ✔ ....

2 Jenny is shortest girl in our class. ✗ Jenny is the shortest girl in our class.

3 I am the young child in my family. ☐ ....

4 Are cheetahs the faster animals in the world? ☐ ....

5 I think History is the most interesting subject. ☐ ....

6 What is the bad song in the world? ☐ ....

7 Grandpa is the oldest man in our family. ☐ ....

8 Maths is the good subject at school. ☐ ....

9 Comparative or superlative

11 **Write than or the.**

1 My brother is braver _than_ me.

2 Paris is .... most beautiful city in the world.

3 Chocolate is nicer .... cabbage.

4 Saturday is .... best day of the week.

5 I'm short but Bob is .... shortest.

6 Football is more exciting .... tennis.

7 Are you .... cleverest student in your class?

8 CDs are more expensive .... books.

9 This is .... nicest café in the town.

10 I'm better at dancing .... my brother.

12 **Look and write.**

1 Tony / short / Mike   Tony is shorter than Mike.

2 Sally / tall   Sally is the tallest.

3 Mike / old / Tony

4 Jenny and Sally / old

5 Tony / young

6 Sally / heavy / Tony

7 Mike / light

8 Tony / short

Name	Age	Height	Weight
Tony	10	1 m 48 cm	55 kilos
Sally	12	1 m 72 cm	58 kilos
Mike	11	1 m 65 cm	46 kilos
Jenny	12	1 m 57 cm	62 kilos

13 **Read, choose and write.**

Amy: I'm hungry. What's for dinner?

Emma: Mum's making stew with potatoes and cabbage.

Amy: Oh no! Cabbage is the (**1**) ...._worst_.... food in the world.

Emma: No, it isn't. It's very good for you.

Amy: Chocolate is the (**2**) .... food. It's the (**3**) .... delicious food in the world.

Emma: Well, you need fruit and vegetables, too. They're the most (**4**) .... foods of all.

Amy: They're the (**5**) .... boring foods of all, too.

Emma: Don't be silly. Fruit and vegetables make you healthy and strong.

Amy: I'm the (**6**) .... person in the family and I'm the (**7**) .... runner in my class.

Emma: You aren't faster than me.

Amy: Yes, I am! You're (**8**) .... than everybody!

Emma: No, I'm not! Come on! Let's race to the kitchen! The winner can have lots of cabbage!

1	bad	worse	worst
2	best	better	good
3	most	than	more
4	tasty	important	nicest
5	most	than	more
6	strong	stronger	strongest
7	fast	faster	fastest
8	slow	slower	slowest

(14) Write.

Monday

Dear Diary,

Today was my first day at my new school. My new school is bigger **(1)** ...than... my old school. There are lots of children there. My new classroom is **(2)** .... nicest classroom in the school. It's **(3)** .... modern than my old classroom. There are lots of computers and the desks are newer **(4)** .... the desks at my old school. The **(5)** .... exciting part of the day was when I made a new friend. His name is James. He's very tall. He's **(6)** .... than our teacher! He's very funny, too. He's **(7)** .... funniest boy in my class. I played with James at lunch time and he's coming to my house tomorrow! I'm the happiest boy **(8)** .... the world!

(15) Rewrite correctly.

1 I'm the ~~younger~~ person in my class.   I'm the youngest person in my class.

2 My dad is the cleverest person ~~than~~ my family. ....

3 Are you ~~tallest~~ than your brother? ....

4 Sharks are ~~most~~ dangerous than dolphins. ....

5 This is the ~~more~~ expensive jacket in the shop. ....

6 Jenny is ~~happiest~~ than she was yesterday. ....

7 You are the ~~funnier~~ boy in the class. ....

8 Everest is the tallest mountain ~~than~~ the world. ....

(16) What about you? Choose and write.

young   old   clever   tall   short   fast
beautiful   ugly   small   big   new   nice

1 I / person in my class   I'm the shortest/youngest person in my class.

2 I / than my friend   I am taller/older than my friend.

3 my friend / in the school   ....

4 my friend / me   ....

5 I / person in my family   ....

6 my house / than my friend's house   ....

7 my teacher / teacher in the school   ....

8 my bedroom / than the living room   ....

Fun Grammar Review ④

① Choose and write.

his   ~~hers~~   ours   our   your   theirs   mine   yours

1 That's Susie's laptop. It's _hers_ .
2 These are our sweets. They're ....
3 John's got a car. Look at .... car.
4 This is your belt. It's ....

5 We've got new bikes. Those are .... bikes.
6 This is their torch. It's ....
7 Those are my CDs. They're ....
8 You've got a nice house. I like .... house.

② Rewrite correctly.

1 This red and blue jacket is ~~my~~.   This jacket is mine.
2 Are those ~~yours~~ new trainers?   ....
3 Those bikes over there are ~~their~~.   ....
4 Is this ~~hers~~ compass or John's?   ....
5 That's ~~ours~~ lovely dog.   ....
6 Are those ~~theirs~~ school books?   ....
7 The red bag on the desk is ~~him~~.   ....
8 That's ~~mine~~ pencil case.   ....
9 Those dirty jeans are ~~Sam~~.   ....
10 ~~Who~~ pencil is this, please?   ....

③ Write.

Adjective	Comparative	Superlative
fast	faster	the fastest
nice		
happy		
big		
good		
bad		
beautiful		
intelligent		
silly		
young		
tall		

4 **Write the correct form.**

Jake: What are you doing, Tina?

Emma: I'm watching *Our Family*. It's (**1**) ...... the funniest ...... (funny) show on TV.

Jake: Really? Is it (**2**) .... (good) than *Strange Street?*

Emma: Yes, it is. It's got (**3**) .... (good) actor in the world.

Jake: Who's that?

Emma: Donny Klepp, of course! He's (**4**) .... (amazing) person on TV.

Jake: I don't know him.

Emma: What? But he's (**5**) .... (famous) actor of all.

Jake: I don't watch a lot of TV. I think listening to music is (**6**) .... (exciting) than watching TV.

Emma: I like music, too. Have you got lots of CDs?

Jake: I usually listen to MP3s. They're (**7**) .... (cheap) than CDs.

Emma: Have you got an MP3 player?

Jake: Yes, I have. It's new. It was (**8**) .... (expensive) MP3 player in the shop.

Emma: Wow! It's (**9**) .... (nice) than mine. It's very small, too.

Jake: I know. It's (**10**) .... (small) than my mobile phone. I can take it everywhere.

Emma: Cool!

5 **Choose and write.**

more   biggest   their   our   me   ours   ~~hotter~~   us

Dear Karen,

I'm in Spain! It's very hot here. It's (**1**) ...... hotter ...... than England. We're staying in a very big hotel. It's the (**2**) .... hotel in the town. The rooms are very modern and they're (**3**) .... comfortable than my bedroom at home! My brother and I are in one room and (**4**) .... parents are in another room. My parents are lucky. (**5**) .... room is bigger than (**6**) .... I go to the beach every morning. My brother comes with (**7**) .... We swim in the sea and we play volleyball in the water. Mum bought (**8**) .... a beach ball, so we're very happy.

See you soon!

Lisa

My English

You are on holiday. Write a letter to your friend about it.

Dear .... ,

I'm in .... ! It's very .... It's .... than .... We're staying in .... hotel. It's the .... in the town. I go .... Dad bought .... a ....
I'm very happy.

See you soon!

....

10 -*ing* forms, infinitive forms
-*ing* forms

We use the -ing form of a verb like a noun.
We use the -ing form as the subject of a sentence.
   Skateboarding is fun.

We use the -ing form after adjectives with prepositions.
   I'm good at skiing.   He's scared of travelling by plane.

We use the -ing form after these verbs: like, enjoy, hate, love
   We love swimming.

We also use the -ing form with What about …? to make suggestions.
   What do you want to do today?   What about surfing?

Look! Spelling rules
   write → writing   run → running

① Write.

1 I love ....surfing........ (surf).

2 Bob is good at .... (rock climb).

3 Do you like .... (fish)?

4 What about .... (play) my new computer game this afternoon?

5 I'm scared of .... (swim) in the sea.

6 .... (dance) makes us happy.

7 .... (eat) lots of chocolate is bad for you.

8 Did you enjoy .... (watch) the football game?

② Choose and write the correct form.

come   ~~go~~   wear   watch   dance   listen

CARNIVAL TIME!

Do you love (**1**) ....going........ to parties? What about (**2**) .... to the best party in town!

Everybody enjoys (**3**) .... the parade and we all love (**4**) .... to the wonderful music.

Are you good at (**5**) ....? Why not join in the dance competition!

So put on your costume and join us! Everybody loves (**6**) .... amazing costumes.

So come on! The carnival is great!

3 Look and write.

	ice skate	fish	cycle	surf
Amy	☺☺	☹	☺	☺
Tom	☺	☹	☺☺	☺

☹ = hate
☺ = like
☺☺ = love

1 Amy / ice skate   *Amy loves ice skating.*

2 Tom / cycle   ....

3 Amy and Tom / surf   ....

4 Tom / ice skate   ....

5 Amy and Tom / fish   ....

6 Amy / cycle   ....

4 Write and match.

1 Jake likes ...... *reading* ...... (read)   **a** football.

2 He enjoys .... (watch)   **b** books.

3 He is good at .... (play)   **c** mountains.

4 He is scared of .... (climb)   **d** TV.

5 He hates .... (walk)   **e** pasta.

6 He loves .... (eat)   **f** the dog.

5 What about you? Write.

1 I / like   *I like skateboarding.*   4 I / scared of ....

2 I / enjoy ....   5 I / hate ....

3 I / good at ....   6 I / love ....

6 What about you? Write the questions and answers.

1 you / good at / dance?   *Are you good at dancing?*
Yes, I am./No, I'm not.

2 your friend / like / ice skate?   *Does your friend like ice skating?*
....

3 you / enjoy / travel by train? ....
....

4 you / scared of / swim / in the sea? ....
....

5 your friend / like / play football? ....
....

6 you / love / cycle? ....
....

47

10 Infinitive forms

> We use to + the infinitive form of the verb after the verb want.
>   I want to go to the party.
>   I don't want to stay at home.
>
> We also use to + the infinitive form of the verb to say why we did something.
>   I went to the supermarket to buy some milk.

7 Choose and write the correct form.

ride   ~~buy~~   do   make   visit   walk   go   play

1 My brother Dan wants ......to buy...... some new jeans at the shops today.

2 Look! It's raining. We don't want .... to school today. Let's go in the car.

3 I want .... a cake for Emma's birthday. She's 10 years old today.

4 Ben wants .... his new bike in the park. Can you take him, Dad?

5 Mum doesn't want .... to the supermarket this afternoon. She's busy.

6 The children don't want .... their History homework.

7 I want .... basketball with my friends after school today.

8 My cousin wants .... me next weekend. He can sleep in my room.

8 Match and write.

1 He went to the bank
2 We bought some flowers
3 I made some sandwiches
4 She went to the post office
5 They went to the garage
6 We visited the art gallery
7 I bought a new T-shirt
8 He bought some spaghetti

a .... (look) at some paintings.
b .... (hire) a car.
c ......to get...... (get) some money.
d .... (give) to grandma.
e .... (cook) for dinner.
f .... (wear) to the party.
g .... (send) a letter.
h .... (eat) on our picnic.

9 What about you? Answer.

1 What do you do today?   I want to ....

2 Who do you want to do visit this weekend? ....

3 Where do you want to go today? ....

4 Why do you go to school? ....

Infinitive or -ing

(10) Write the correct form.

1 Do you like ___watching___ (watch) scary films?

2 I don't want ___to go___ (go) to the museum tomorrow.

3 We enjoyed _____ (play) volleyball at the beach.

4 Does Mark want _____ (come) to the park with us?

5 Are your friends good at _____ (skateboard)?

6 Dad wants _____ (take) me to the zoo tomorrow.

7 The children want _____ (stay) up late tonight.

8 She isn't scared of _____ (travel) by helicopter

(11) Read, choose and write.

Tom: Hi, Amy. What are you doing?

Amy: I'm making a costume for the fancy dress party tomorrow. I'm good at (1) ___making___ costumes.

Tom: Really? I want (2) _____ to the party but I don't want (3) _____ a costume.

Amy: Why not? (4) _____ up is lots of fun.

Tom: No, it isn't. I hate (5) _____ costumes. I look silly.

Amy: No, you don't. What about (6) _____ a prince?

Tom: No, I don't want (7) _____ a prince.

Amy: Well, what about a superhero?

Tom: Hmm … a superhero is a good idea.

Amy: OK. I'm happy you want (8) _____ a superhero costume to the party.

Tom: Really? Do you want (9) _____ me?

Amy: Of course. I enjoy (10) _____ people.

Tom: Wow! Thanks, Amy.

1	make	making	to make
2	to go	go	going
3	wear	to wear	wearing
4	Dress	To Dress	Dressing
5	to wear	wearing	wear
6	to be	being	be
7	to be	being	be
8	wear	to wear	wearing
9	help	to help	helping
10	help	to help	helping

(12) Write the correct form.

Dear Emma,

How are you? I'm having a great time in Turkey. We go to the beach every day. I love (1) ___swimming___ (swim) in the sea. I like (2) _____ (walk) on the beach, too. The food here is delicious. I enjoy (3) _____ (try) new foods. I know some words in Turkish now. I want (4) _____ (learn) some more words, because I'm good at (5) _____ (speak) different languages. I want (6) _____ (go) to the shops now. I want (7) _____ (buy) some presents for my friend. I love (8) _____ (shop)!

See you soon!

Amy

11 Future forms
going to

We use going to to talk about our plans for the future.
   I'm going to visit my friend tomorrow.

We also use going to to make a prediction, when something we see in the present tells us that something is going to happen in the future.
   The sky is very dark. There's going to be a storm.

We often use these time expressions with going to:
   today, tomorrow, next Monday/weekend/week/month/year

Affirmative
I'm going to dance.
He/She/It's going to dance.
Tou/We/They're going to dance.

Negative
I'm not going to dance.
He/She/It isn't going to dance.
You/We/They aren't going to dance.

Questions
Am I going to dance?
Is he/she/it going to dance?
Are you/we/they going to dance?

Short answers
Yes, I am.   No, I'm not.
Yes, he/she/it is.   No, he/she/it isn't.
Yes, we/you/they are.   No, we/you/they aren't.

Wh- questions
What am I going to do today?
Where is he/she/it going to go tomorrow?
Who are you/we/they going to see next weekend?

① **Write the correct form.**

1 I ___'m going to meet___ (meet) my friends after school today.

2 Ben _____ (not play) football tomorrow. He's ill.

3 We _____ (go) on holiday next month.

4 It's eight o'clock. You _____ (be) late for school.

5 _____ (you/do) your homework today?

6 They _____ (not visit) their cousins next weekend.

7 I'm making sandwiches. I _____ (have) a picnic in the park.

8 Lisa's at the cinema. She _____ (watch) a film.

9 The sun is shining. It _____ (be) a lovely day today.

10 _____ (it/rain) today? The sky looks cloudy.

I'm going to go to a party tomorrow.

2 Look and write.

John	Kate	Billy and Joe	Susie	Tina	Paul

1 John / be / a singer

John isn't going to be a singer. He's going to be a painter.

2 Kate / travel / to Argentina

....

3 Billy and Joe / go / rock climbing

....

4 Susie / meet me / at the museum

....

5 Tina / visit / her cousin

....

6 Paul / eat / spaghetti

....

3 Write the correct form.

Emma: Hi, Jake. What are you doing?

Jake: I'm putting all my things in boxes.
I (**1**) 'm going to move .... (move)
to my new house next week.

Emma: Wow! (**2**) .... (you/live)
in a new town?

Jake: No, (**3**) .... I (**4**) .... (live) near
the school.

Emma: (**5**) .... (you/have) a bigger bedroom.

Jake: Yes, (**6**) .... (**7**) .... (Dad/buy) me
a new bed and a desk.

Emma: Cool.

Jake: (**8**) .... (I/paint) my new bedroom blue and
(**9**) .... (Mum/give) me some new posters for my birthday.

Emma: That's great. (**10**) .... (you/have) a really cool room.

Jake: I know. I can't wait!

We use will to say what we think, predict or know will happen in the future.
   I think it will rain later.

We also use will when we talk about doing something at the moment we decide to do it.
   The phone is ringing. I'll answer it.

We often use these time expressions with will:
   later, one day, in the future, when I'm older, in five/ten/twenty years

Affirmative	**Negative**
I/You/He/She/It/We/They will sing.	I/You/He/She/It/We/They won't (will not) sing.

Questions	**Short answers**
Will I/you/he/she/it/we/they sing?	Yes, I/you/he/she/it/we/they will.
	No, I/you/he/she/it/we/they won't.

Wh- questions
What will I/you/he/she/it/we/they sing?

---

4 **Match and write.**

1 I'm good at acting.
2 You sing very well.
3 Peter is good at painting.
4 Emma likes helping people.
5 It's my birthday next Friday.
6 My friend and I love animals.
7 Mark and Lisa are good at sport.
8 The clouds are very black.

a .... (it/be) an amazing day.
b .... (they/be) famous footballers one day.
c .... (we/be) vets in a zoo when we're older.
d *I'll be* (I/be) a famous actress one day.
e .... (you/be) a pop star when you're older.
f .... (he/be) a great artist one day.
g .... (she/be) a doctor when she's older.
h .... (it/rain) later this afternoon.

5 **Choose and write.**

take   have   wear   make   answer   ~~close~~   buy   watch   read   go

1 It's cold in here. I *'ll close* the window.

2 We're hungry. I .... some sandwiches.

3 It's Lucy's birthday. I .... her a present.

4 It's raining. I .... my umbrella.

5 This book looks good. I .... it.

6 It's very hot today. I .... my shorts.

7 I feel ill. I .... to the doctor's.

8 I'm thirsty. I .... some orange juice.

9 The phone is ringing. I .... it.

10 There's a good film on TV. I .... it.

6 **Look and write. Use will or won't.**

When John is older …

1 he / be a doctor

He won't be a doctor.

2 he / drive a fast car

3 he / live in a small house

4 he / be a footballer

5 he / ride a scooter

6 he / win lots of prizes

7 **What about you? Write the questions and answers.**

1 you / be / a doctor / when you're older

Will you be a doctor when you're older?   Yes, I will. / No, I won't.

2 you drive / a fast car / in the future

3 you live / in a small house / in the future

4 you / be / a footballer / one day

5 you ride / a scooter/ in the future

6 you / win / lots of prizes / one day

8 **Circle.**

Amy: I'm writing about life in the future for my homework.

Tom: Really? What (**1**) will / won't life be like in the future?

Amy: I think it will (**2**) be / being very different. We'll have flying cars (**3**) in / one day.

Tom: Wow. Where (**4**) will / do we live?

Amy: We'll live in big houses. But the houses (**5**) will / won't be on Earth. They'll be in space.

Tom: (**6**) Are / Will we have computers?

Amy: Yes, we (**7**) Will / won't .

Tom: Will the computers be big, too?

Amy: No, they (**8**) will / won't . They'll be very small.

Fun Grammar Review (5)

① Circle.

1 I don't like to play / (playing) computer games.
2 Do you want to watch / watching a film with me?
3 Emma loves to ski / skiing in the mountains.
4 We want to go / going to the beach tomorrow.

5 Are you good at to write / writing stories?
6 Katie is scared of to ride / riding scooters.
7 The boys don't want to go / going to bed.
8 Ben likes to talk / talking to his friends.

② Write the correct form.

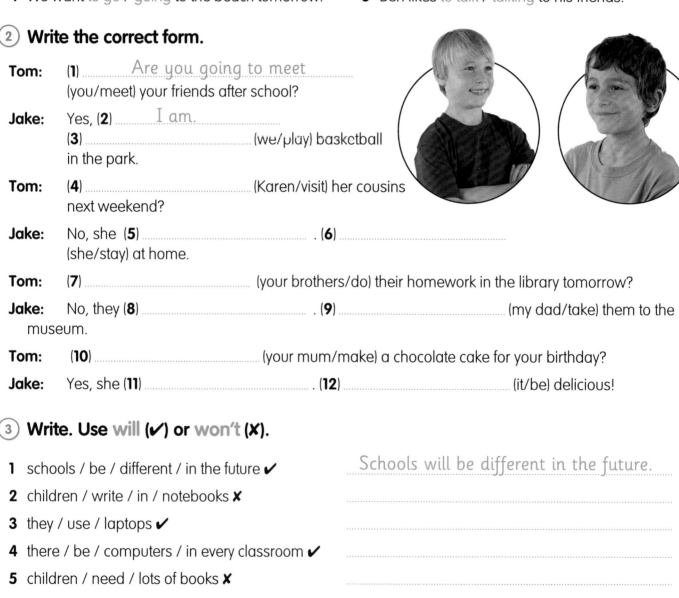

Tom: (1) _____Are you going to meet_____ (you/meet) your friends after school?

Jake: Yes, (2) _____I am._____
(3) _____ (we/play) basketball in the park.

Tom: (4) _____ (Karen/visit) her cousins next weekend?

Jake: No, she (5) _____ . (6) _____ (she/stay) at home.

Tom: (7) _____ (your brothers/do) their homework in the library tomorrow?

Jake: No, they (8) _____ . (9) _____ (my dad/take) them to the museum.

Tom: (10) _____ (your mum/make) a chocolate cake for your birthday?

Jake: Yes, she (11) _____ . (12) _____ (it/be) delicious!

③ Write. Use will (✔) or won't (✗).

1 schools / be / different / in the future ✔
2 children / write / in / notebooks ✗
3 they / use / laptops ✔
4 there / be / computers / in every classroom ✔
5 children / need / lots of books ✗
6 they / read / information / on the Internet ✔

Schools will be different in the future.

4 Read, choose and write.

Dear Mike,

Thanks for your email. You've got lots of exciting plans for the future! I want (**1**) ....to be.... a doctor when I'm older. I'm good at (**2**) .... science and I love (**3**) .... people. I want (**4**) .... in a big hospital in the city because I like (**5**) .... busy. I'll live in a big house with a garden and all my friends (**6**) .... visit me every weekend. It'll be great. I think I (**7**) .... need good grades to be a doctor, so I (**8**) .... to work very hard. I've got lots of homework to do tonight, so I'll start now!

Write soon!

Tony

1	will be	to be	being
2	will learn	learning	to learn
3	to help	will help	helping
4	to work	working	will work

5	to be	will be	being
6	will	are	won't
7	going to	will	to
8	will	won't	'm going

4 What about you? Answer.

1 What do you want to be when you are older?   I want to be ....

2 What are you good at? ....

3 What do you love doing? ....

4 Where will you work in the future? ....

5 Where will you live in the future? ....

6 Will you need good grades to do your future job? ....

My English

Write an email to your friend about your plans for the future.

Dear .... ,

Thanks for your email. Your plans for the future are very exciting. I've got lots of plans, too. I want ....
....

I'm good at ....
I will ....
....

See you soon!

....

12 Present perfect

We use the present perfect to talk about things we did in the past that have a result in the present.

We've tidied the living room. (The living room is tidy now.)

We use has/have + past participle of the verb to form the present perfect.
The past participles of regular verbs are the same as the past simple forms.

play → played → played

The past participles of irregular verbs are different. Each verb has its own past participle.

see → saw → seen   fall → fell → fallen
go → went → been   swim → swam → swum
hear → heard → heard   speak → spoke → spoken
have → had → had   know → knew → known
drive → drove → driven take → took → taken

See a full list of irregular past participles on p96.

Affirmative
He/She/It has eaten.
I/You/We/They have eaten.

Negative
He/She/It hasn't eaten.
I/You/We/They haven't eaten.

Questions
Has he/she/it eaten?
Have I/you/we/they eaten?

Short answers
Yes, he/she/it has.   No, he/she/it hasn't.
Yes, I/we/you/they have.   No, we/you/they haven't.

Wh- questions
What has he/she/it seen?
Where have I/you/we/they been?
Who has he met?

① **Write.**

Verb	Past simple form	Past participle
do	did	done
make	made	
catch	caught	
feed	fed	
drink	drAnk	
have	had	
ride	rode	
meet	met	
eat	ate	
sing	sang	

2 Choose and write.

1 I've _been_ to the supermarket.

    a go   **b** went   **c** ~~been~~

2 She's .... the dog for a walk.

    a take   **b** taken   **c** took

3 We've .... to our teacher.

    a spoken   **b** spoke   **c** speak

4 He's .... an email to his cousin.

    a write   **b** wrote   **c** written

5 I've .... a glass.

    a broke   **b** broken   **c** break

6 They've .... their kites in the park.

    a flown   **b** fly   **c** flew

7 She's .... her homework.

    a done   **b** do   **c** did

8 They've .... to school.

    a went   **b** gone   **c** go

3 Write and match.

1 He _'s bought_ (buy) some bread.

2 I .... (close) the window.

3 We .... (do) our homework.

4 She .... (find) her keys.

5 You .... (lose) your mobile phone.

6 They .... (spend) all their money.

7 I .... (drink) a lot of water.

8 You .... (buy) a new dress.

a She can open the door now.

b He can make some sandwiches now.

c They can't buy an ice cream now.

d It's warmer in here now.

e You can't call your friends now.

f We can play computer games now.

g You look lovely.

h I'm not thirsty now.

4 Choose and write the correct form.

drink   finish   ~~wash~~   cook   do   feed   buy   see   eat   read

1 I _'ve washed_ the kitchen floor. It's clean now.

2 We .... the dog. It isn't hungry now.

3 You .... all the milk. There isn't any milk for me.

4 He .... dinner. It looks delicious.

5 They .... their English lesson. They can leave the classroom now.

6 I .... a new CD. Grandma gave me the money.

7 She .... her magazine. She's going to read a book now.

8 You .... your lunch. Was it nice?

9 I .... all my homework. Can I watch TV now?

10 We .... that film. Let's watch a different one.

5 Choose and write the correct form.

make   put   paint   speak   give   hear   clean   ~~be~~

Dear Helen,

How are you? I **(1)** ___have been___ very busy this week. My friends and I are starting a Kids Club at our school. It's a place for children to meet after school. Our teacher **(2)** _____ us the keys to an empty classroom. The room was very dirty, but we **(3)** _____ the walls and the floor now. We **(4)** _____ the walls yellow and orange and we **(5)** _____ lots of cool posters on the walls. My dad is good at making things and he **(6)** _____ a big table for the room. I **(7)** _____ to our teacher and she's going to come to the club every day. Lots of children **(8)** _____ about the club and they all want to join. Will you join, too?

Write soon,

Emma

6 Write the correct form.

1 I _'ve washed_ the dishes but I _haven't washed_ the car. (wash)

2 He _____ his pizza but he _____ his chips. (eat)

3 You _____ your bedroom but you _____ the living room. (tidy)

4 They _____ some milk but they _____ any bread. (buy)

5 She _____ the newspaper but she _____ the magazine. (read)

6 We _____ to the bank but we _____ to the post office. (be)

7 I _____ to my cousin but I _____ to my grandma. (write)

8 He _____ his teeth but he _____ his hair. (brush)

7 Write.

Jack's to do list

tidy my room	✗
buy some tomatoes	✔
wash the dishes	✗
do my homework	✔
help dad in the garden	✔
phone my friend	✔
have a guitar lesson	✗
meet my cousin	✗

1 Jack hasn't tidied his room.

2 He's _____

3 _____

4 _____

5 _____

6 _____

7 _____

8 _____

8 **Match and write.**

1 ___Have___ you brushed your teeth, Penny?

2 _____ they finished their homework?

3 _____ she cleaned the floor?

4 _____ the cat eaten the fish?

5 _____ we broken the window?

6 _____ he been shopping?

a No, it _____ .

b Yes, they _____ .

c No, we _____ .

d Yes, he _____ .

e No, I ___haven't___ .

f Yes, she _____ .

9 **Write the questions and answers.**

Today				Diary		
Anna	✔	✔	✘	✘	✔	✘
Sam	✘	✔	✘	✔	✘	✔

1 Anna / go / to the post office?   Has Anna gone to the post office?   Yes, she has.

2 Sam / go / to the post office _____

3 Anna and Sam / polish / their shoes? _____

4 Anna / write / in her diary? _____

5 Sam / have a shower? _____

6 Sam / gone / horse riding? _____

7 Anna and Sam / eat / lunch? _____

8 Sam / write / in his diary? _____

10 **Write the correct form.**

Jake: Hi, Emma. **(1)** ___Have you lost___ (you/lose) something?

Emma: Yes, I have.

Jake: Oh dear. **(2)** _____ (what/you/lose)?

Emma: My mobile phone **(3)** _____ (disappear).

Jake: **(4)** _____ (you/look) under your bed?

Emma: Yes, I have. It isn't there.

Jake: **(5)** _____ (you/leave) it at school?

Emma: No, I haven't. **(6)** _____ (I/not/use) it this evening. I phoned Amy at five o'clock.

Jake: OK. Let's think. **(7)** _____ (where/you/be) this evening?

Emma: **(8)** _____ (I/not/be) anywhere. I stayed in my bedroom all evening.

Jake: **(9)** _____ (who/be) in your bedroom this evening?

Emma: Nobody has been in here. Oh, wait! My brother was here!

Jake: **(10)** _____ (your brother/take) your mobile phone?

Emma: Yes, he has! Listen! I can hear him talking on the phone! Come on! Let's go and talk to him!

12   *yet*

We use yet in negative sentences and questions when we talk about recent actions with the present perfect. Yet comes at the end of the sentence or question.
> I haven't had my breakfast yet.
> Have you cleaned your teeth yet? Yes, I have.

11 Write sentences with yet.

1 We can't go to the park.

We haven't finished our homework yet.
(we / not finish / our homework)

2 Dan isn't ready for school.

....
(he / not have / a shower)

3 There isn't any food in the fridge.

....
(we / not go / to the supermarket)

4 I bought this book yesterday.

....
(I / not read / it)

5 Karen isn't at my house.

....
(she / not arrive)

6 Mark isn't ready for his holiday.

....
(he / not pack / his suitcase)

12 Look, choose and write.

get up   ~~brush hair~~   make breakfast   ~~make coffee~~   eat breakfast
wash dishes   get dressed   feed the cat   clean the floor   open the window

1 She hasn't brushed her hair yet.   6 ....

2 She has made coffee.   7 ....

3 ....   8 ....

4 ....   9 ....

5 ....   10 ....

13 Match and write.

1 **Mum:** Have you spoken to John yet? **Dad:** _Yes, I have._   **a** He left at nine o'clock.

2 **Mum:** Has Tom gone to the bank yet? **Dad:** ....   **b** It's really dirty.

3 **Mum:** Have you had lunch yet? **Dad:** ....   **c** They're making lunch now.

4 **Mum:** Has Jenny arrived yet? **Dad:** ....   **d** I phoned him last night.

5 **Mum:** Have the boys eaten yet? **Dad:** ....   **e** I ate a sandwich.

6 **Mum:** Have you washed the car yet? **Dad:** ....   **f** She's very late.

14 Write the correct form.

Dear Sam,

Can you come to my house today? My cousins are coming to visit today, and I want you to meet them. There are lots of things to do before they get here. Mum (**1**) _has gone_ (go) to the supermarket but she (**2**) .... (not cook) dinner yet. Dad (**3**) .... (paint) the fence but he (**4**) .... (not cut) the grass yet. I (**5**) .... (tidy) the living room but I (**6**) .... (not wash) the kitchen floor yet. I (**7**) .... (not brush) my hair yet but I (**8**) .... (have) a shower. Luckily, my cousins (**9**) .... (not arrive) yet! (**10**) .... (you/buy) that new computer game yet? If you have, please bring it so we can play.

See you soon!

Lisa

15 What about you? Write the questions and answers.

1 brush / your hair

   Have you brushed your hair yet?   _Yes, I have. / No, I haven't._

2 have / a shower

   ....

3 cook / dinner

   ....

4 tidy / the living room

   ....

5 wash / the kitchen floor

   ....

6 go / to the supermarket

   ....

13 Present perfect
Have you ever?

We use the present perfect to talk about events or actions in the past but we don't say exactly when the event or action happened.
> I've visited London.

We use the present perfect to talk about recent experiences or the things we have done or haven't done in the past.
> I've been to France.
> I haven't ridden a horse.

We can use Have you ever? to ask questions about past or recent experiences.
> Have you ever met a famous actor? Yes, I have.

① **Look and write.**

	Tom	Amy	Emma and Jake	You
climb a mountain	✔	✘	✘	
swim in a lake	✘	✔	✘	
visit a castle	✔	✘	✔	
ride a horse	✘	✔	✔	

1 Tom / climb / a mountain   Tom has climbed a mountain.

2 Amy / visit / a castle   ....

3 Emma and Jake / swim / in a lake   ....

4 Tom / ride / a horse   ....

5 Amy / climb / a mountain   ....

6 Emma and Jake / visit / a castle   ....

What about you? Complete the table and write.

1 ....

2 ....

3 ....

4 ....

2 Write.

1 I / be / to New York ✔   I've been to New York.

2 my teacher / ride / a motorbike ✘   My teacher hasn't ridden a motorbike.

3 my friend / swim / with dolphins ✘ ....

4 They / fly / in a plane ✔ ....

5 my friends / be / canoeing ✘ ....

6 Sandra / sleep / in a tent ✔ ....

7 my cousin / see / a polar bear ✔ ....

8 We / go / horse riding ✘ ....

3 What about you? Write the questions and answers.

1 you / be / to New York   Have you ever been to New York?   No, I haven't. / Yes, I have.

2 you / fly / in a plane ....

3 you / be / canoeing ....

4 you / sleep / in a tent ....

5 you / see / a polar bear ....

6 you / go / horse riding ....

4 Write the correct form.

Tom: I'm really excited! I'm going on a boat trip tomorrow.
(**1**) __Have you ever been__ (you/ever/be) on a boat trip?

Amy: No, I haven't. You're very lucky.

Tom: We're going to travel to the river by train.
(**2**) .... (you/ever/travel) by train?

Amy: No, I haven't. But I (**3**) .... (watch) the trains at the station.

Tom: We're going to catch fish in the river. (**4**) .... (you/ever/catch) a fish?

Amy: No, I haven't. I (**5**) .... (not do) many things.

Tom: (**6**) .... (you/ever/swim) in a river?

Amy: No, I haven't. But I (**7**) .... (play) in the sea.

Tom: I'm going to swim in the river tomorrow. Mum (**8**) .... (buy) me a new swimming costume.

Amy: I (**9**) .... (read) about that river on the Internet. There are crocodiles in it.
(**10**) .... (you/ever/see) a crocodile?

Tom: No … I haven't seen a crocodile … yet.

13 Present perfect or past simple

We use the present perfect to talk about past experiences and events, but we don't say exactly when those experiences or events happened.

I've been to New York.

We also use the present perfect to talk about something that started in the past but has a connection to the present.

Harry's gone to New York. (He left in the past but he's still there.)

We use the past simple to talk about past experiences and events and we say when those experiences or events happened.

I went to New York in 2005.
We visited Grandma last weekend.

5 Write.

1 I ....went.......... (go) to the museum last Sunday.

2 Ben .... (not finish) his food yet.

3 .... (you/ever/see) a snake?

4 We .... (visit) our friend Kate yesterday.

5 .... (Katie/come) home from school yet?

6 We .... (watch) a film last night.

7 .... (Sam/ever/stay) in a hotel?

8 You .... (send) me a letter last week.

9 We .... (not go) to Paris last year.

10 I .... (buy) a car in 2009.

6 Write the correct form.

(1) ....Have you ever wanted.... (you/ever/want) to live in space? Lots of astronauts (2) .... (travel) into space. The first person (3) .... (go) into space in 1961. His name was Yuri Gargarin. (4) .... (you/ever/hear) of Neil Armstrong? In 1969 he (5) .... (walk) on the moon. People all over the world (6) .... (see) Neil on television that day. The Americans and the Russians (7) .... (build) lots of space rockets. They (8) .... (learn) a lot about other planets, too. Nobody (9) .... (live) on another planet yet, but a lot of people (10) .... (think) about it!

(7) Look and write.

	Billy	Jess	Mary and Jill
visit Russia	last year	last year	last week
fly in a helicopter	in 2009	last July	in 2008
meet a famous singer	last month	last week	in 2009
swim with dolphins	in 2008	in 2007	last year

1 Billy / visit / the USA?

Has Billy ever visited the USA? Yes, he has. He visited Russia last year.

2 Jess / fly / in a helicopter?

....

3 Mary and Jill / swim / with dolphins?

....

4 Billy / meet / a famous singer?

....

5 Jess / visit / Russia?

....

6 Mary and Jill / meet / a famous singer?

....

7 Billy / fly / in a helicopter?

....

8 Jess / swim / with dolphins?

....

(8) Rewrite correctly.

1 Has Tom ever ~~was~~ to a concert? Has Tom ever been to a concert?

2 We ~~seen~~ a great play last week. ....

3 Our teacher has ~~rode~~ a motorbike. ....

4 Did you ~~swum~~ in the sea last summer? ....

5 I haven't ~~did~~ my homework yet. ....

6 We ~~gone~~ rock climbing last weekend. ....

7 Have you ~~wrote~~ an email to your cousin? ....

8 Jenny ~~eaten~~ a sandwich for lunch yesterday. ....

Fun Grammar Review (6)

(1) Write the correct form.

1 I ___'ve washed___ (wash) the kitchen floor. It's clean now.

2 We ___haven't fed___ (feed) the dog. It's hungry.

3 You _____ (drink) all the milk. There isn't any milk for me.

4 He _____ (cook) the dinner. We've got nothing to eat.

5 They _____ (finish) their English lesson. They're in their lesson now.

6 I _____ (buy) a new CD. It's great!

7 _____ (she/read) her magazine? She looks bored.

8 You _____ (eat) your lunch. You will be hungry later.

9 _____ (you/do) your homework? It's time for bed.

10 It _____ (start) to rain. Now we can't go out.

(2) Write.

Verb	Past simple	Past participle
look	**(1)** looked	looked
eat	ate	**(2)**
(3)	went	gone
catch	**(4)**	caught
run	ran	**(5)**
ride	rode	**(6)**

(3) Write the correct form.

1 She ___has lost___ her keys. She ___lost___ them yesterday. (lose)

2 I _____ John. I _____ him last Friday. (meet)

3 Katie _____ at the airport. She _____ at four o'clock. (arrive)

4 We _____ a new car. We _____ it last week. (buy)

5 You _____ this joke. You _____ it last night. (hear)

6 They _____ dinner. They _____ at half past seven. (eat)

7 I _____ that book. I _____ it last month. (read)

8 You _____ in this hotel. You _____ here last year. (stay)

(4) Read, choose and write.

Saturday

Dear Diary

I'm in New York! I **(1)** _'ve been_ here a day now. It's a really amazing place! I've **(2)** .... very busy and I've done lots of exciting things. I **(3)** .... the Statue of Liberty and I've **(4)** .... lots of photos. I **(5)** .... been on a boat trip yet. I'm going to do that tomorrow. I've been to the shops and I **(6)** .... some souvenirs. I've walked in Central Park and I've **(7)** .... in a horse and carriage, too! I haven't been to the theatre **(8)** .... but I've got tickets for a show on Saturday. I've **(9)** .... lots of great food, too. I **(10)** .... to a wonderful restaurant last night and I had steak and chips. It was delicious!

1 been	be	've been		**6** buy	've bought	've buy
2 be	were	been		**7** ridden	ride	rode
3 've visited	's visited	hasn't visited		**8** yesterday	yet	ever
4 took	take	taken		**9** eat	ate	eaten
5 have	haven't	hasn't		**10** go	went	been

(5) What about you? Answer.

1 What amazing place have you visited? ....

2 What did you do there? ....

3 Have you ever been on a boat trip? ....

4 Have you ever ridden in a horse and carriage? ....

5 Have you ever been to the theatre? ....

6 Have you ever been to a restaurant? ....

My English

Imagine you are on holiday. Write in your diary about what you have done and haven't done yet.

Saturday

Dear Diary,

I'm in .... ! I've been here .... I've been very busy and I've done lots of things. I've ....

I haven't ....

I've ....

....

14 Modal verbs 1
can, could

Modal verbs always stay the same. We don't add -s to modal verbs for he/she/it.
I can ride a horse. He can ride a horse.
We use an infinitive without to after a modal verb.
I can swim.
We don't form questions with do/does or did with modal verbs.
Can you dance?

We use can/can't to talk about ability in the present.
He can surf.
We can't skateboard
Can she rollerblade? Yes, she can.

We use could/couldn't to talk about ability in the past.
I could swim when I was five.
He couldn't go to the party last Saturday.
Could you talk when you were a baby? No, I couldn't.

1 Write **can** or **can't**.

1 ...Can... Emma sing? Yes, she ...can... .
2 .... you ride a horse? No, I ....
3 .... Mike speak Italian? No, he ....
4 .... the girls dance? Yes, they ....
5 .... your dog swim? Yes, it ....
6 .... you and Dan ski? No, we ....

2 Write **could** or **couldn't**.

1 I ...couldn't... talk yesterday because I had a sore throat.
2 .... you swim when you were six years old? No, I couldn't.
3 Lisa lived in France when she was little. She .... speak French then.
4 He .... go to school last Monday because he had a cold.
5 Could Tom walk when he was two years old? Yes, he ....
6 We .... have a picnic in the park last weekend because it was raining.

3 Look and write.

Jenny	ride a bike	skateboard	sing	play tennis
5 years old	✘	✘	✔	✘
now	✔	✘	✘	✔

1 ride a bike _Jenny couldn't ride a bike when she was five. She can ride a bike now._
2 skateboard ....
3 sing ....
4 play tennis ....

must, mustn't

We use must/mustn't to talk about rules.
> You mustn't run in the classroom.

We use must to say that something is necessary.
> You must do your homework.

We use must not/mustn't to tell somebody not to do something.
> You mustn't be late for school.

We don't usually use must/mustn't in questions.

---

(4) Write must or mustn't.

1 I ...mustn't... be late for school.

2 We .... be quiet in lessons.

3 You .... do your homework.

4 He .... be rude to the teacher.

5 They .... listen in class.

6 I .... write on the desk.

7 She .... talk on her mobile phone in lessons.

8 You .... bring your notebook to school.

These are our school rules.

---

(5) Write.

These are the park rules.

Park rules

Please keep the park tidy.
Don't leave toys in the park.
Please put litter in the bin.
Don't ride your bike on the grass.
Don't swim in the pond.
Please keep your dog with you.
Don't climb the trees.
Please leave the park at 11pm.

1 You must keep the park tidy.

2 ....

3 ....

4 ....

5 ....

6 ....

7 ....

8 ....

14 have to, don't have to

We use have to/has to to say that something is necessary.
    We have to brush our teeth every day.
We use don't have to/doesn't have to to say that something is not necessary.
    You don't have to clean the floor. I cleaned it this morning.

Have to changes in the third person.
    I/You/We/They have to go to school.   He/She/It has to go to bed.

With have to, we form questions with do/does and we form negatives with don't/doesn't
    Do you have to tidy your room? Yes, I do./No, I don't.
    He doesn't have to wash the dishes.

6 Write the correct form.

1 I .... *have to* .... help my dad today. He's got lots of work to do.

2 He .... clean his bedroom today. He cleaned it yesterday.

3 You .... brush your teeth before you go to bed.

4 They .... do their homework today. They did it yesterday.

5 She .... go to the supermarket. She hasn't got any food.

6 I .... stay at home today. I can go to the beach.

7 Look and write.

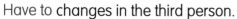

Sam's list

write an email to my cousin	✗
tidy the living room	✔
do my homework	✗
help Mum in the kitchen	✔
phone my grandma	✔
walk the dog	✗

1 Sam doesn't have to write an email to his cousin.

2 He has to ....

3 ....

4 ....

5 ....

6 ....

8 Write the questions and answers.

1 ...... Do you have to ...... (you/tidy) your bedroom? ...... Yes, I do .... It's a mess!

2 .... (he/wash) the car? .... He washed it yesterday.

3 .... (they/phone) their cousins? .... They phoned them this morning.

4 .... (she/clean) the floor? .... She hasn't cleaned it yet.

5 .... (we/go) to school today? .... It's the school holidays.

6 .... (you/buy) Tom a present? .... It's his birthday tomorrow.

can, could, must, mustn't, have to or don't have to

⑨ Read, choose and write.

Emma: What are you doing, Amy?

Amy: I'm doing my Maths homework. I (**1**) ......*couldn't*...... do it last night because I was tired.

Emma: Oh no! You (**2**) .... do your homework now. We'll be late for school.

Amy: But I (**3**) .... to finish it. I don't want my teacher to be angry.

Emma: Oh, OK. (**4**) .... I help you?

Amy: No, don't worry. You (**5**) .... to help me. I'll be OK.

Emma: Don't be silly. You're my friend. I want to help.

Amy: Well, I've done these questions but this one is really difficult. I (**6**) .... do it.

Emma: Oh, I had a problem with that question, too. I (**7**) .... do it last night but I suddenly knew the answer this morning.

Amy: Great! (**8**) .... you show me how to do it?

Emma: Sure. But we (**9**) .... go now. We (**10**) .... be late.

Amy: Thanks, Emma. You're a star!

1	can't	could	couldn't	**6**	can	could	can't
2	must	have to	mustn't	**7**	couldn't	could	can't
3	has to	have to	mustn't	**8**	Must	Do	Can
4	Can	Could	Must	**9**	must	could	has to
5	have to	mustn't	don't have to	**10**	have to	mustn't	couldn't

⑩ Write.

1 Do ..*have*.. you to go to school on Sundays?

2 Tim is clever. He .... read when he was four.

3 I .... ride a bike, but I can't ride a horse.

4 .... Jenny have to tidy her room today?

5 .... you speak English when you were six?

6 You .... your homework before you watch TV.

7 I .... go to school last week. I was ill.

8 You .... have to cook. I've got pizza.

⑪ Rewrite correctly.

1 We ~~doesn't~~ have to clean the floor today.   We don't have to clean the floor today.

2 I ~~can~~ ride a bike when I was four years old.   ....

3 We ~~couldn't~~ go to the party tomorrow.   ....

4 You ~~must~~ be late for school.   ....

5 Becky ~~have~~ to look after her little sister today. ....

6 ~~Can~~ you run when you were two years old?   ....

7 ~~Does~~ you have to tidy your bedroom?   ....

8 He doesn't ~~has~~ to help his dad today.   ....

15 Modal verbs 2
Let's, Shall?, Would you like?

We use Let's, Shall? and Would you like? to make suggestions.
> Let's go to the beach.
> Shall we take some sandwiches?
> Would you like to come with us?

We also use shall to ask for advice or to offer help.
> What shall I wear to the party?
> Shall I wash the dishes?

1 Write. Use Let's.

~~buy him a present~~   go tobogganing   go to the beach   run
go to bed   go to the shop   help her   take an umbrella

1 It's Mike's birthday. _Let's buy him a present._   **5** It's going to rain. ....

2 Mum is very busy. ....   **6** We're tired. ....

3 We're late. ....   **7** It's hot today. ....

4 It's snowing. ....   **8** There's no milk. ....

2 Choose and write. Use shall.

~~I go~~   I open   I call   we make   we do   I wash

1 'There's no food in the fridge.'
' _Shall I go_ to the supermarket?'

2 'What .... for dinner?'
'What about cooking spaghetti?'

3 'It's hot in here.'
' .... the window?'

4 'What .... this evening?'
'Let's watch a film.'

5 'I'm bored.'
' .... our friends?'

6 'That was a lovely meal.'
' .... the dishes?'

3 Write let's, shall or would.

Jake: I'm going to the cinema next Saturday. (**1**) _Would_ you like to come?
Tom: Yes, please. I love films. (**2**) .... I bring a friend?
Jake: That's a good idea.
Tom: I can bring my cousin, Olga.
Jake: I don't know Olga.
Tom: She's at my house today. (**3**) .... go there so you can meet her.
Jake: OK. But it's nearly lunch time. What (**4**) .... we eat?
Tom: (**5**) .... get some pizza on the way to my house.
Jake: Good idea.
Tom: I've got another idea too. Olga and I play basketball together every Thursday. (**6**) .... you like to play with us?
Jake: I'd love to! That's a great idea.

should, shouldn't

We use should/shouldn't to give and ask for advice.
   You should work hard at school.
   You shouldn't eat lots of chocolate.
   Should I stay up late tonight? No, you shouldn't.

We can also use modals with Wh- questions.
   What should I buy Sam for his birthday?
   You should buy him a T-shirt.

④ **Choose and write. Use should or shouldn't.**

go   talk   ~~listen~~   wear   play   see

1 Jake: I've got a headache.
   Mum: You _shouldn't listen_ to loud music.

2 Jake: I'm tired.
   Dad: You .... to bed early tonight.

3 Jake: I don't feel well.
   Mum: You .... a doctor.

4 Jake: The teacher shouted at me today.
   Mum: You .... in class.

5 Jake: I've got lots of homework today.
   Mum: You .... computer games.

6 Jake: My face is red from the sun.
   Mum: You .... sun cream.

⑤ **Look and write.**

~~eat a lot of sweets~~   eat fruit and vegetables   walk or cycle to school   play computer games all day
do lots of sports   listen to very loud music   have breakfast every day   sit on the sofa all the time

1   Children shouldn't eat a lot of sweets.

2   They should ....

3   ....

4   ....

5   ....

6   ....

7   ....

8   ....

16 Sentence linking
and, or, but

We use and to link two statements which talk about similar actions or situations.
We don't have to repeat the subject pronoun in the second statement.

I went shopping. I bought a T-shirt.
I went shopping and (I) bought a T-shirt.

We use or to link two statements which talk about two possible actions or situations.

We can eat now. We can eat later.
You can eat now or we can eat later.

We use but to link two statements which talk about different actions or situations.

I like chocolate. I don't like cheese.
I like chocolate but I don't like cheese.

① Circle.

1 He plays the guitar (and) / but writes his own songs.

2 I can ride a bike and / but I can't drive a car.

3 You shouldn't run but / and shout in the library.

4 We can play now but / or we can play later.

5 I watch funny films or / but I don't watch scary films.

6 She likes comics and / but loves books.

7 They can ski and / but they can ice skate.

8 He hates skateboarding and / but he likes skiing.

② Write and, or or but.

Emma: I'm doing a project about elephants. Look, I've got a photo.

Jake: Are you writing it on paper (**1**) ......or...... are you working on your laptop?

Emma: I have to do it on paper.

Jake: OK. Well. Did you know that elephants can run (**2**) .... they can swim?

Emma: Really? What do elephants eat?

Jake: They eat grass (**3**) .... they don't eat meat.

Emma: Great. Where do elephants live?

Jake: They live in Africa (**4**) .... they live in India.

Emma: Have they got big ears (**5**) .... have they got small ears?

Jake: They've got big ears. African elephants have got the biggest ears. They've got a long nose too called a trunk. They can move trees (**6**) .... they can carry heavy things with their trunks.

Emma: Wow! Elephants are very strong. Thanks for the help, Jake.

when

We use when to talk about the time of an event, feeling or action.
I'm happy when I'm surfing.
I wear my jacket when it's cold.

③ Match.

1 I take my umbrella when
2 Mum always makes us food when
3 I never go to school when
4 We usually go to the park when
5 She wears sun cream when
6 The children do their homework when
7 He watches TV when
8 I make a cake for my grandma when

a they come home from school.
b we want to play football.
c she goes to the beach.
d it's raining.
e there's a good film on.
f she comes to visit me.
g we're hungry.
h I'm ill.

④ Write.

1 We eat ice cream. It's hot and sunny.
2 He's got free time. He phones his friends.
3 I'm happy. I'm playing computer games.
4 She watches TV. Her mum says she can.
5 They buy CDs. They have some money.
6 I listen to loud music. I get a headache.
7 It's snowing. We go tobogganing.
8 I get a stomach ache. I eat too much.

We eat ice cream when it's hot and sunny.
He phones his friends when he's got free time.
....
....
....
....
....
....

⑤ Write and, or, but or when.

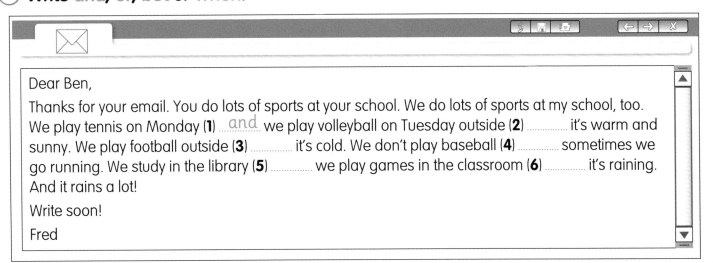

Dear Ben,

Thanks for your email. You do lots of sports at your school. We do lots of sports at my school, too.
We play tennis on Monday (1) ...and... we play volleyball on Tuesday outside (2) .... it's warm and
sunny. We play football outside (3) .... it's cold. We don't play baseball (4) .... sometimes we
go running. We study in the library (5) .... we play games in the classroom (6) .... it's raining.
And it rains a lot!

Write soon!

Fred

16 First, Then, Next, Finally

We use First, Then, Next and Finally to talk about the order of events.

First I got out of bed. Then I went down the stairs. Next I ate my breakfast. Finally I went to school.

6 Circle.

How to make a sandwich
This is my favourite sandwich. (**1**) Next / First you take some bread. (**2**) Then / Finally you put some butter, cheese, tomatoes and crisps on the bread. (**3**) First / Next you put another piece of bread on top. (**4**) First / Finally you eat your delicious sandwich!

How to make a mask
It's easy to make a mask. (**5**) First / Next you cut holes for your eyes. (**6**) Finally / Then you paint your mask. (**7**) Next / First you put some string on your mask. (**8**) Finally / First you wear your mask to a fancy dress party!

7 Look, choose and write.

have / a picnic   meet / their friends   make / some sandwiches   walk / to the park

Yesterday Wendy and Charlie spent the day together. First they made ....

....

....

....

Why? Because

We use why to ask for reasons.
Why were you late?
Why don't you like snakes?

We use because to give reasons.
Because the bus was late.
Because they're scary.

⑧ Write why or because.

Amy: Hi, Tom. **(1)** ......Why...... are you late?

Tom: **(2)** .... I was tired. I stayed up late last night.

Amy: Oh dear. **(3)** .... didn't you go to bed early?

Tom: I didn't go to bed early **(4)** .... there was a funny film on TV.

Amy: Well, I've been here a long time. **(5)** .... didn't you call me?

Tom: **(6)** .... I lost your mobile number. I'm sorry, Amy. I ran here very fast.

Amy: But **(7)** .... didn't you catch the bus?

Tom: **(8)** .... I haven't got any money.

Amy: Oh, Tom! You had some money yesterday. **(9)** .... haven't you got any money now?

Tom: **(10)** .... I bought this T-shirt. Do you like it?

Amy: Yes, it's great. But you're very silly! Come on, let's go to the park!

⑨ Write the questions and answers.

1 You didn't go to the party yesterday.

I / be / ill

Why didn't you go to the party yesterday?
Because I was ill.

2 Ben isn't watching the film now.

he / do / his homework

3 The children haven't got up yet.

they / be / very tired

4 Katie plays tennis every day.

she / like / sport

5 You aren't eating your dinner now.

I / not be / hungry

6 They aren't going to come to my party next Friday.

they / visit / their cousins

Fun Grammar Review ⑦

① Circle.

1 You should / (shouldn't) play computer games all day.

2 I must / mustn't do my homework.

3 He has to / doesn't have to wear a jacket. It's warm today.

4 She can / can't go to the party. She's ill.

5 We could / couldn't do our homework because it was very difficult.

6 They should / shouldn't go to bed. They're very tired.

7 We have to / don't have to go to school in the holidays.

8 You must / mustn't be rude to people.

② Write and match.

1 Mark doesn't ...have... to feed the cat.

2 Katie .... skateboard.

3 I .... talk when I was one year old.

4 What .... we do tomorrow?

5 .... you like to come to the cinema?

6 We .... eat sweets now.

a Let's go to the beach.

b His mum fed it this morning.

c It's time for dinner

d There's a great film on today.

e She can ice skate, too

f I was a very clever baby.

③ Choose and write.

~~First~~   and   Then   or   Finally   but

Jake: Hi, Emma. I'm making a pizza.

Emma: I love pizza! How do you make it?

Jake: (1) ...First... you need some pizza bread. I bought this bread at the supermarket.

Emma: Cool.

Jake: (2) .... you put tomatoes on the bread (3) .... you put cheese on top of the tomatoes.

Emma: Are you going to put chicken on the pizza (4) .... are you going to put peas?

Jake: Peas? You don't put peas on pizza. I'll add chicken.

Emma: I like peas (5) .... I don't like chicken.

Jake: OK. I won't put any chicken on it. Let's put more cheese on it.

Emma: What do you do now?

Jake: (6) .... you cook the pizza for twenty minutes.

Emma: That's easy! You're a great cook, Jake.

Jake: Thanks.

4 Match.

1 Why didn't you do your homework?
2 Why didn't you call me?
3 Why is it cold in here?
4 Why isn't Mark at school today?
5 Why is the house a mess?
6 Why are your clothes wet?

a Because it's raining.
b Because we had a party last night.
c Because my mobile phone is broken.
d Because he's got a cold.
e Because I left my books at school.
f Because the window is open.

5 Choose and write.

should   Why   and   can   but   Shall   would   when

Dear Peter,

Thanks for your email. (1) ...Why... are you worried about your school work? You're good at Maths
(2) .... you're great at English. You don't like Art (3) .... you're very good at this subject, too.
OK, you're having problems with History. But I've got some advice. First you (4) .... talk to your
teacher. She (5) .... help you with your problems. Then you should go to the library. There
are some good History books there. (6) .... I meet you there on Saturday? It's easy to study
(7) .... you're with a friend. I've been to the library before and I can show you the books. What
time (8) .... you like to meet?

See you soon!

Tom

My English

Your friend wants some help at school. Write him/her an email giving advice and making suggestions.

Dear .... ,

Thanks for your email. Why are you worried about your school work? You're good at ....
OK, you're having problems with .... But I've got some advice.
First ....

....

....

....

See you soon!

....

I can do this! 1

1 Circle.

1 We buy / (bought) a fish at the pet shop yesterday.

2 I 'm painting / paint a picture of a storm now.

3 They see / saw lots of fish at the aquarium last weekend.

4 There was / were lots of people outside the town hall yesterday.

5 My dad is a policeman. He works / worked at the police station.

6 I eat / ate chips at the café last Sunday.

7 You 're writing / write in your diary every day.

8 We're visit / visiting the museum today.

2 Write the correct form.

Tom: Hi, Amy. What (**1**) ....are you doing....... (you/do) in town today?

Amy: Hi, Tom. Mum and I (**2**) .... (buy) some clothes for our holiday. I usually (**3**) .... (go) shopping on Saturday but Mum (**4**) .... (be) always busy at the weekends.

Tom: I see. Are you going to Italy again?

Amy: Yes, we are. We (**5**) .... (go) to Italy every year. We always (**6**) .... (stay) in a hotel near the beach.

Tom: Cool. My family and I (**7**) .... (visit) Italy last summer. It (**8**) .... (be) very hot and sunny.

Amy: (**9**) .... (you/eat) lots of ice cream?

Tom: Yes, I (**10**) .... Italian ice cream is great!

3 Look at Exercise 2. Answer.

1 Are Amy and her mum buying clothes?   Yes, they are.

2 Does Amy's mum go shopping at the weekends?

3 Does Amy go to Italy every year?

4 Do Amy and her mum stay in a tent?

5 Did Tom visit Spain last summer?

6 What did Tom eat in Italy?

4 **What about you? Answer.**

1 What do you usually do on Saturday? ....

2 What are you doing now? ....

3 Are you always busy at the weekends? ....

4 Where do you usually go on holiday? ....

5 Where did you go last year? ....

6 What did you eat? ....

5 **Write one word in each gap.**

Hi Jane,

How are you? (**1**) ..... Are ..... you enjoying your weekend? (**2**) .... the sun shining? What (**3**) .... you usually do at the weekends? Do you (**4**) .... in the sea? I'm a very good swimmer but I (**5**) .... usually swim in the sea. I like swimming pools. There's a swimming pool near my house and I go there at the (**6**) .... Last weekend my little brother came to the pool, too. We had lots of fun. My mum and dad usually (**7**) .... me to the pool but they didn't take me last weekend. My grandpa (**8**) .... me. I was happy. Grandpa always buys us ice creams after we swim!

Write soon,

Lisa

6 **Write an email to your friend. Say what you usually do at the weekend and what you did last weekend.**

Hi .... ,

How are you? Did you have a good weekend? I had a great weekend. I usually .... on Saturdays but last Saturday I ....

On Sundays I usually ....

but last Sunday ....

....

Write soon!

I can do this! 2

1 **Write.**

Subject pronouns	Object pronouns
I	**(1)** me
you	**(2)**
he	**(3)**
she	**(4)**
it	**(5)**
we	**(6)**
you	**(7)**
they	**(8)**

2 **Write.**

Possessive adjectives	Possessive pronouns
my	**(1)** mine
your	**(2)**
(3)	his
(4)	hers
(5)	–
our	**(6)**
(7)	yours
their	**(8)**

3 **Choose and write.**

any   few   ~~your~~   my   me   yours
lot   some   mine   little

Emma: Hi, Jake. I'm sorry I didn't come to **(1)** your birthday party
yesterday. Did you have a good day?

Jake: Yes, thanks. I got a **(2)** .... of great presents.

Emma: Really? What did you get?

Jake: My mum and dad bought me a **(3)** .... CDs and my grandma
and grandpa gave me **(4)** .... money.

Emma: That's nice. Was this laptop a birthday present, too?

Jake: No, it wasn't. That laptop isn't **(5)** .... It's my dad's laptop.

Emma: Oh, I see. Is this compass **(6)** .... ?

Jake: Yes, it is. It was a present from **(7)** .... brother.

Emma: Great!. Did you get **(8)** .... birthday cards?

Jake: Yes, I did. And my mum made **(9)** .... a big cake. There's
a **(10)** .... cake in the kitchen. Do you want a piece?

Emma: Ooh, yes, please!

(4) Circle.

1 We haven't got (much) / many milk.

2 There are a few / little cherries in the bowl.

3 My brother goes to your school. Do you know he / him?

4 We've got new bikes. Those bikes are our / ours.

5 She bought some / any spaghetti at the supermarket.

6 Are those steaks for us / we?

7 They've got a dog. That dog is their / theirs.

8 There were a lot / little of people in the park yesterday.

(5) Read, choose and write.

Saturday

Dear Diary,

I went shopping with (1) ___my___ my friends today. There weren't (2) _____ people in town. It was very quiet. We visited (3) _____ favourite shops and we bought a (4) _____ of cool things. I didn't have (5) _____ money but I bought a (6) _____ cheap T-shirts. My friend Lucy bought a CD and she bought (7) _____ beautiful flowers for (8) _____ mum. My friend Ben bought a present for (9) _____ brother. Then we met my mum and she took (10) _____ to a café. It was a great day.

1	me	my	mine	**6** few	little	lot
2	much	many	lot	**7** some	any	no
3	us	our	ours	**8** she	her	hers
4	little	few	lot	**9** him	his	he
5	much	many	little	**10** we	us	our

(6) You went shopping yesterday. Write in your diary. Say what you and your friends bought.

Saturday

Dear Diary,

I went shopping with my friends yesterday. We visited _____ .

I bought _____ .

My friend _____ .

My friend _____ .

Then, we _____ .

It was _____ .

I can do this! 3

1 Write.

Adjective	Comparative	Superlative
fast	faster	the fastest
big		
nice		
happy		
good		
bad		

2 Circle.

1 Lions are (bigger) / biggest than cats.

2 Laptops are more expensive / most expensive than radios.

3 I think summer is the better / best season of the year.

4 John and Dave are the funnier / funniest boys in my class.

5 Dad is the worse / worst dancer in my family.

6 Cars are more / most comfortable than motorbikes.

7 My teacher is the nice / nicest teacher in the school.

8 Dolphins are more beautiful / the beautiful than sharks.

3 Read, choose and write.

Jake: Happy birthday, Emma. How old are you today?
Emma: I'm twelve.
Jake: Wow. You're (**1**) ....older.... than me. I'm eleven.
Emma: Yes, but you're (**2**) .... than me. I'm the (**3**) .... person in my class.
Jake: Never mind. You're the (**4**) .... girl in the class, too.
Emma: Thanks, Jake. You're the (**5**) .... person in the world!
Jake: Are you having a (**6**) .... party for your birthday?
Emma: No, I'm not. I'm taking a few friends to the (**7**) .... pizza restaurant in town.
Jake: Wow. That's great.
Emma: I know. They make the (**8**) .... pizza in the world. Do you want to come?
Jake: Yes, please!

1	old	older	oldest
2	tall	taller	tallest
3	short	shorter	shortest
4	pretty	prettier	prettiest
5	nice	nicer	nicest
6	big	bigger	biggest
7	good	better	best
8	delicious	more delicious	most delicious

4 Write one word in each gap.

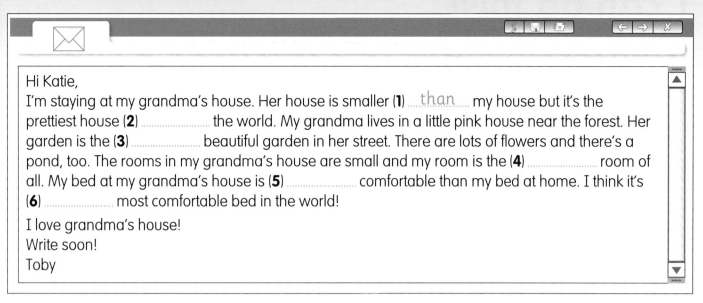

Hi Katie,

I'm staying at my grandma's house. Her house is smaller (**1**) ....*than*.... my house but it's the prettiest house (**2**) .... the world. My grandma lives in a little pink house near the forest. Her garden is the (**3**) .... beautiful garden in her street. There are lots of flowers and there's a pond, too. The rooms in my grandma's house are small and my room is the (**4**) .... room of all. My bed at my grandma's house is (**5**) .... comfortable than my bed at home. I think it's (**6**) .... most comfortable bed in the world!

I love grandma's house!
Write soon!
Toby

5 What about you? Answer.

1 Is your house bigger than your friend's house? ....

2 Who's got the most comfortable bed in your house? ....

3 Is your house the prettiest house in the street? ....

4 What's the smallest room in your house? ....

5 Is your bed the most comfortable in the house? ....

6 You are visiting your cousin. Write an email to your friend. Say what is different about your cousin's house and your house.

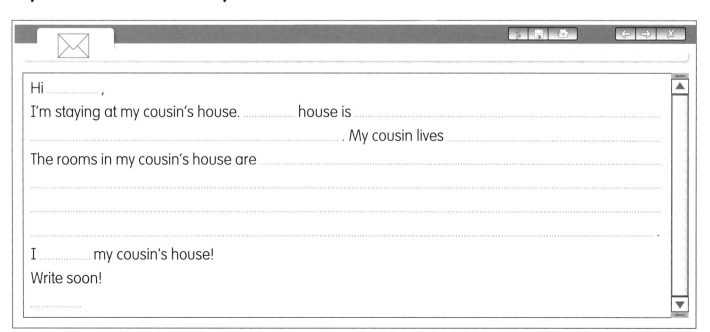

Hi .... ,

I'm staying at my cousin's house. .... house is ....
.... My cousin lives ....
The rooms in my cousin's house are ....
....
....
....

I .... my cousin's house!
Write soon!
....

I can do this! 4

① Circle and match.

1 Do you want (to watch) / watching
2 I don't like to play / playing
3 Mark enjoys to walk / walking
4 What about to go / going
5 Mum went to the market to buy / buying
6 We love to listen / listening
7 The children want to stay / staying
8 I went to my bedroom to do / doing

a volleyball.
b some fruit.
c up late tonight.
d my homework.
e a film with me?
f to music.
g in the mountains.
h to the beach this weekend?

② Write the correct form.

Tom: Hi. I'm going skateboarding. Do you want (1) ....to come.... (come) with me?

Amy: No, thanks. I don't like (2) .... (skateboard).

Tom: Oh. Well, what do you want (3) .... (do)?

Amy: I'm not sure. Do you like (4) .... (play) tennis?

Tom: Not really. I enjoy (5) .... (watch) tennis but I don't want (6) .... (play) it.

Amy: OK. What about (7) .... (go) to town?

Tom: Oh, no. I went to town yesterday (8) .... (buy) some new school books. I don't want (9) .... (go) again today.

Amy: Well, what about (10) .... (stay) here? I've got a new DVD.

Tom : That's a good idea. Let's stay here.

③ Write the correct form.

I'm Dean and I love (1) ......acting...... (act). I first wanted (2) .... (be) in a play when I was eight years old. At primary school, my teacher wanted (3) .... (find) somebody for the school play *Aladdin*. He chose me! It was fun.

I enjoy (4) .... (do) sport too. I like (5) .... (play) volleyball and I'm good at (6) .... (swim). I like (7) .... , (run) in races, but I hate (8) .... (lose)! But I love (9) .... (be) in plays the most and one day I want (10) .... (be) an actor.

4 **What about you? Answer.**

1 What do you love doing? _I love_ ....

2 What do you hate doing? ....

3 What do you like doing the most? ....

4 What do you want to be? ....

5 What are you good at doing? ....

6 What do you enjoy doing? ....

5 **Choose and write.**

playing   to   ~~riding~~   at   about   going   to   want

Hi Tom,

Thanks for your email. You've got lots of great hobbies. I've got lots of hobbies, too. I like
(**1**) _riding_ my bike in the park and I love (**2**) .... tennis. It's my favourite sport. I want (**3**)
.... be in the school tennis club next year. I'm very good (**4**) .... playing tennis but I'm
better at playing basketball. I go to the sports centre (**5**) .... play basketball every Friday. I
love (**6**) .... to the sports centre with my friends. I enjoy swimming, too. I (**7**) .... to go to
the beach next weekend. Do you like swimming? What (**8**) .... coming with me?

Write soon!

Lisa

6 **Write an email to your friend about your free time. Say what you like doing, what you are good at and what you want to do next weekend.**

Hi .... ,
Thanks for your email. You've got a lot of hobbies. I've got lots of hobbies, too. I love ....
....
I'm good at ....
....
Next weekend I want to ....
....
Write soon!
....

I can do this! 5

① Write. Use going to.

Jake: This is a great football game. Our team are playing really well.

Tom: I know. They (**1**) .... are going to win .... (win).

Jake: I love football. I (**2**) .... (join) the team next year.

Tom: That's a great idea. You're really good at football. My sister and I (**3**) ....
(start) tennis lessons next year but we (**4**) .... (not/have) our lessons
at school. We (**5**) .... (join) the sports centre.

Jake: Cool. I (**6**) .... (go) swimming at the sports centre this weekend. Do you
want to come, too?

Tom: I can't. I (**7**) .... (visit) my grandparents this weekend. They
(**8**) .... (take) me to the zoo.

Jake: That's nice.

Tom: Oh dear. Look at those clouds. (**9**) .... (it/rain)?

Jake: Yes, it is. But don't worry. I've got my umbrella. We (**10**) .... (not/get) wet.

② Write the questions and answers.

Monday:	go swimming
Tuesday:	meet Sally
Wednesday:	have a guitar lesson
Thursday:	buy some new shoes
Friday:	play tennis
Saturday:	visit my cousins
Sunday:	go to the cinema

1 What / Emma / do / on Monday?

What's Emma going to do on Monday?   She's going to go swimming.

2 Who / Emma / meet / on Tuesday?

....

3 When / Emma / have / a guitar lesson?

....

4 What Emma / buy / on Thursday?

....

5 When / Emma / play / tennis?

....

6 Who / Emma / visit / on Saturday?

....

7 Where / Emma / go / on Sunday?

....

3 **Write. Use will or won't.**

Nobody knows what life **(1)** .... *will be* .... (be) like in the future but some people think that we **(2)** .... (live) on another planet one day. In 1969 the first man walked on the moon but living on another planet is still a dream. People **(3)** .... (travel) to Venus, because the air on Venus is dangerous. They **(4)** .... (go) to Mercury because it's very close to the sun. But one day people **(5)** .... (go) to Mars because it's safe there. It **(6)** .... (happen) soon because travelling to space is very expensive and difficult. But people **(7)** .... (visit) Mars one day and maybe some brave people **(8)** .... (stay) there.

4 **Write one word in each gap.**

Monday

Dear Diary,

I'm going on holiday with my family tomorrow! We're going to go to Spain! We're **(1)** ..... *going* ..... to travel there by plane. I'm going to **(2)** .... up very early tomorrow because we're going to leave the house **(3)** .... eight o'clock. I think the weather will **(4)** .... nice in Spain. I'll swim in the sea every day and I **(5)** .... eat a lot of ice cream. Mum and Dad **(6)** .... going to take their cameras because they are **(7)** .... to take lots of photos. I'm going **(8)** .... take my camera, too. It **(9)** .... be boring. It will be great! I think we **(10)** .... have a great time. I can't wait!

5 **You are going on holiday next week. Write in your diary. Say what you are going to do and what you think will happen on your holiday.**

Monday

Dear Diary,

My family and I are going on holiday next week. We're going to ....

....

I think ....

I'm going to ....

I think ....

I can do this! 6

1 **Write the correct form.**

Gorillas live in mountains and forests. Sadly, many gorillas
(**1**) ....._have lost_..... (lose) their homes because people
(**2**) .... (cut) down the trees in the forests. Some
people from zoos (**3**) .... (make) a new home
for gorillas. These zoos are often beautiful places Zaire,
Jookie and Effie are gorillas who (**4**) .... (go) live
in a zoo in London. Effie is the oldest gorilla. She
(**5**) .... (live) in Germany and the UK. Zaire
(**6**) .... (not/live) in Germany but she
(**7**) .... (stay) in zoos in the USA and the UK. She's
a very friendly gorilla and she (**8**) .... (find) a lot
of friends at the zoo. Jookie (**9**) .... (be) at the
zoo for two years. She's cute. This zoo (**10**) ....
(have) lots of visitors this year. People want to see gorillas
because they are beautiful, clever animals.

2 **Look at Exercise 1. Write the questions and answers.**

1 what / gorillas lose   What have gorillas lost?   They've lost their homes.

2 Who / make a home / for them? ....

3 Who / go to live in London? ....

4 Where / Effie live? ....

5 Where / Zaire stay? ....

6 Who / find a lot of friends? ....

3 **Match.**

1 Have you ever travelled   **a** ever flown in a plane?

2 Who have you   **b** haven't come home yet.

3 John hasn't eaten   **c** to another country?

4 Has she ever ridden   **d** a horse?

5 Have you   **e** any fruit yet.

6 James and Fred   **f** talked to today?

4 Write the correct form.

Amy: What are you doing, Dan?

Dan: I'm playing a computer game.

Amy: (**1**) Have you finished (you/finish) your homework yet?

Dan: Yes, I have. (**2**) .... (do) my homework and I (**3**) .... (tidy) my bedroom.

Amy: Really? (**4**) .... (you/put) all your clothes and books away?

Dan: Yes, I have. I (**5**) .... (be) busy.

Amy: Wow! I'm going to go and look.

Dan: OK. Look! (**6**) .... (you/ ever/see) a tidier bedroom?

Amy: No, I haven't. It's really amazing. You (**7**) .... (not leave) anything on the floor.

Dan: I know!

Amy: (**8**) .... (you/clean) under the bed?

Dan: Wait! Don't look under the bed!

Amy: Oh, Dan! You (**9**) .... (not tidy) your room. You (**10**) .... (put) your clothes and books under the bed!

5 Write one word in each gap.

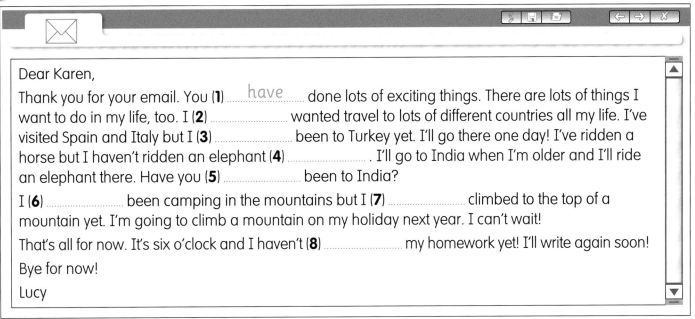

Dear Karen,

Thank you for your email. You (**1**) ...... have ...... done lots of exciting things. There are lots of things I want to do in my life, too. I (**2**) .... wanted travel to lots of different countries all my life. I've visited Spain and Italy but I (**3**) .... been to Turkey yet. I'll go there one day! I've ridden a horse but I haven't ridden an elephant (**4**) .... I'll go to India when I'm older and I'll ride an elephant there. Have you (**5**) .... been to India?

I (**6**) .... been camping in the mountains but I (**7**) .... climbed to the top of a mountain yet. I'm going to climb a mountain on my holiday next year. I can't wait!

That's all for now. It's six o'clock and I haven't (**8**) .... my homework yet! I'll write again soon!

Bye for now!

Lucy

6 Write an email to your friend about your experiences. Say what you have done in your life and what you haven't done yet.

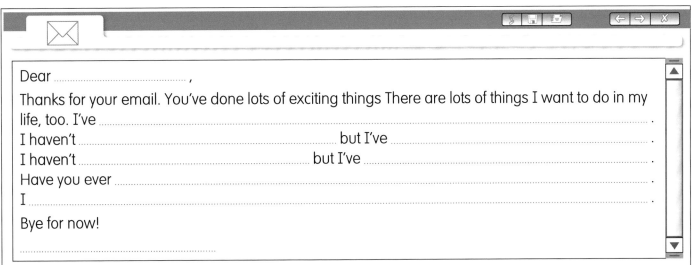

Dear .... ,

Thanks for your email. You've done lots of exciting things There are lots of things I want to do in my life, too. I've ....

I haven't .... but I've ....

I haven't .... but I've ....

Have you ever ....

I ....

Bye for now!

....

I can do this! 7

① Circle.

Doing a sport is good idea. But you (**1**) mustn't / ⟨have to⟩ try hard for some sports. You (**2**) must / mustn't stop doing your sport for a few weeks. You sometimes (**3**) have to / don't have to do it in rainy and sunny weather. You (**4**) can / can't be amazing at first and you (**5**) shouldn't / should practise every week. It's important to eat well, too and you (**6**) mustn't / must eat too many sweets and snacks. But after a few months you will get really good at your sport.

② Choose and write.

1 I _could_ ride a bike when I was five years old.

    a ~~could~~   **b** can   **c** can't

2 You .... stay up late every night.

    a should   **b** shouldn't   **c** have to

3 Children .... go to school.

    a mustn't   **b** don't have to   **c** have to

4 Rabbits ....jump.

    a could   **b** can   **c** can't

5 We .... cross the road when a car is coming.

    a must   **b** mustn't   **c** have to

6 I .... speak English when I was a baby.

    a couldn't   **b** shouldn't   **c** can't

7 You ....brush your teeth every day.

    a could   **b** can   **c** must

8 We .... do any homework in summer.

    a don't have to   **b** couldn't   **c** shouldn't

③ Choose and write.

Let's   shouldn't   doesn't   can   ~~Would~~   can't   have   Shall

Amy: Are you busy, Emma? (**1**) _Would_ you like to come to the park with me?

Emma: I (**2**) .... I've got lots of work to do here. I (**3**) .... to tidy the living room and wash the dishes.

Amy: Oh dear. (**4**) .... I help you?

Emma: Yes, please!

Amy: OK. (**5**) .... tidy the living room first.

Emma: Great. These books and magazines (**6**) .... be here. They are from my bedroom.

Amy: OK. Shall I put them on your shelves?

Emma: Oh, no! You (**7**) .... leave them on my bed. My bedroom (**8**) .... have to be tidy!

Amy: Oh, Emma!

4 Choose and write.

can't   must   ~~can't~~   could   shall   musn't

1   I ____can't____ swim but I can play the piano.

2   Can Dan play football? No, he _____ .

3   You _____ eat sweets. They're bad for your teeth.

4   It's cold. We _____ wear our gloves and scarves.

5   When mum was young she _____ ice skate but now she can't.

6   I'm going camping tomorrow. What _____ I take with me?

5 Circle.

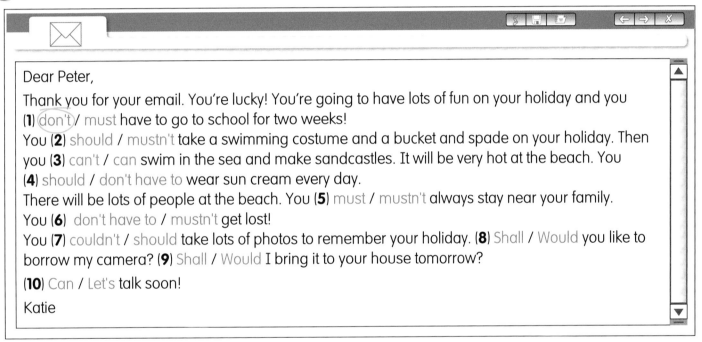

Dear Peter,

Thank you for your email. You're lucky! You're going to have lots of fun on your holiday and you
(1) don't / must have to go to school for two weeks!
You (2) should / mustn't take a swimming costume and a bucket and spade on your holiday. Then
you (3) can't / can swim in the sea and make sandcastles. It will be very hot at the beach. You
(4) should / don't have to wear sun cream every day.
There will be lots of people at the beach. You (5) must / mustn't always stay near your family.
You (6) don't have to / mustn't get lost!
You (7) couldn't / should take lots of photos to remember your holiday. (8) Shall / Would you like to
borrow my camera? (9) Shall / Would I bring it to your house tomorrow?

(10) Can / Let's talk soon!

Katie

6 Your friend is going camping. Write an email to your friend giving advice about what to take and what to do.

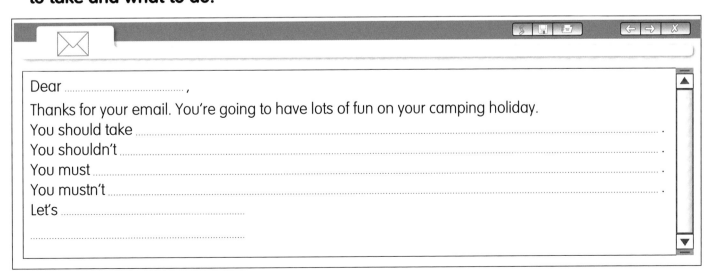

Dear _____ ,
Thanks for your email. You're going to have lots of fun on your camping holiday.
You should take _____ .
You shouldn't _____ .
You must _____ .
You mustn't _____ .
Let's _____
_____

I can do this! 8

1 Circle.

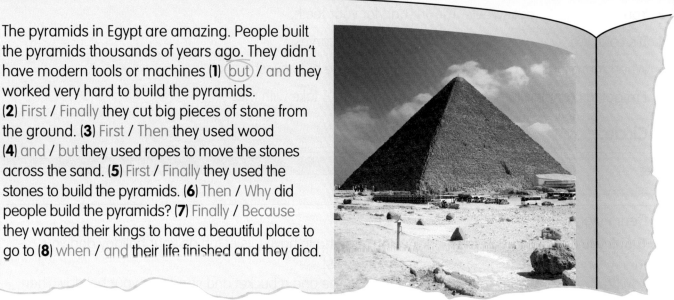

The pyramids in Egypt are amazing. People built the pyramids thousands of years ago. They didn't have modern tools or machines (**1**) (but) / and they worked very hard to build the pyramids.
(**2**) First / Finally they cut big pieces of stone from the ground. (**3**) First / Then they used wood (**4**) and / but they used ropes to move the stones across the sand. (**5**) First / Finally they used the stones to build the pyramids. (**6**) Then / Why did people build the pyramids? (**7**) Finally / Because they wanted their kings to have a beautiful place to go to (**8**) when / and their life finished and they died.

2 Choose and write.

and   but   ~~when~~   First   Then   and   Finally   Because

Amy: You've got lots of books, Tom.

Tom: I know. I read when it's raining and I can't go out. I'm happy (**1**) _when_ I'm reading.

Amy: I like reading (**2**) .... I haven't got many books.

Tom: You can borrow my books.

Amy: Thanks! Is this book good?

Tom: Yes, it is. It's great. I've read the book (**3**) .... I've seen the film. It's about cowboys.

Amy: Oh. I like funny and scary books and films. I don't like books about cowboys (**4**) .... I don't watch cowboy films.

Tom: Why not?

Amy: (**5**) .... they're boring.

Tom: No, they aren't. This story is amazing. (**6**) ...., a cowboy goes to a new town. (**7**) ...., he meets a very bad man. They fight a lot and the cowboy always wins. (**8**) ...., the bad man leaves town.

Amy: Well, I don't have to read the book now. You told me the story!

3 What about you? Answer.

1 Are you happy when you are reading?

Yes, I am./No, I'm not.

2 Do you like books or films?

....

3 What do you do when it's raining?

....

4 Do you like scary films or funny films?

....

4 **Write. Use and or but.**

1 We went to Egypt. We went to France.

We went to Egypt and we went to France.

2 I'm going to swim. I'm not going to play.

....

3 He watched TV. He listened to music.

....

4 You should eat fruit. You shouldn't eat sweets.

....

5 I have to wash the dishes. I have to clean the floor.

....

6 They can't swim. They can surf.

....

5 **Write one word in each gap.**

Sunday

Dear Diary,

I had a wonderful day last Sunday.
(1) First I woke up early and had breakfast with my family. We had eggs on toast
(2) .... we drank orange juice. I love having eggs for breakfast. (3) ....
my Dad took me to the zoo. We saw lions (4) .... we saw elephants. We didn't
see any sharks, (5) .... we saw some dolphins. They were amazing. I was happy
(6) .... a dolphin jumped out of the water in front of me. I took some great
photos. We stayed at the zoo all day. (7) .... Dad took me to my favourite
restaurant for dinner. I had steak and chips. It was delicious! (8) .... we went
home and I went to bed. I was really tired!

6 **Write in your diary. Say what you did last Saturday.**

Sunday

Dear Diary,
I had a wonderful day last Saturday. First I ....

....

Then ....

....

Next ....

....

Finally ....

....

Irregular Verbs

Infinitive	Past simple	Past participle
be	was	been
break	broke	broken
bring	brought	brought
build	built	built
buy	bought	bought
catch	caught	caught
come	came	come
cut	cut	cut
do	did	done
draw	drew	drawn
drink	drank	drunk
drive	drove	driven
eat	ate	eaten
fall	fell	fallen
feed	fed	fed
feel	felt	felt
fight	fought	fought
find	found	found
fly	flew	flown
get	got	got
give	gave	given
go	went	gone
have	had	had
hear	heard	heard
hide	hid	hidden
hold	held	held
keep	kept	kept
know	knew	known

Infinitive	Past simple	Past participle
leave	left	left
let	let	let
lose	lost	lost
make	made	made
meet	met	met
put	put	put
read	read	read
ride	rode	ridden
run	ran	run
see	saw	seen
sell	sold	sold
send	sent	sent
shine	shone	shone
sing	sang	sung
sit	sat	sat
sleep	slept	slept
speak	spoke	spoken
stand	stood	stood
steal	stole	stolen
swim	swam	swum
take	took	taken
teach	taught	taught
think	thought	thought
throw	threw	thrown
wake	woke	woken
wear	wore	worn
win	won	won
write	wrote	written